HORRORS OF HISTORY

CITY OF THE DEAD

T. NEILL ANDERSON

 Charlesbridge

To the city of Galveston and to all who lost their lives
on that terrible Saturday in September

MTM Publishing, Inc.
435 West 23rd Street, #8C
New York, NY 10011
www.mtmpublishing.com

President: Valerie Tomaselli
Series creator: Hilary Poole
Designer: Annemarie Redmond
Illustrator: Richard Garratt
Copyeditor: Sandra Smith
Editorial assistants: Lila Gyory, Anna Luciano

Published by Charlesbridge
85 Main Street
Watertown, MA 02472
(617) 926-0329
www.charlesbridge.com

Library of Congress Cataloging-in-Publication Data
Anderson, T. Neill.
Horrors of history: city of the dead / by T. Neill Anderson.
p. cm.
Summary: The fate of Sam, Charlie, Alice, Daisy, and other Galvestonians hangs in the
balance as the floodwaters rise during the great hurricane that hit Galveston, Texas, in 1900.
ISBN 978-1-58089-514-9 (reinforced for library use)
ISBN 978-1-60734-535-0 (ebook)
ISBN 978-1-60734-603-6 (ebook pdf)
1. Hurricanes—Texas—Galveston—History—20th century—Juvenile fiction. 2. Floods—
Texas—Galveston—History—20th century—Juvenile fiction. 3. Survival—Texas—
Galveston—History—20th century—Juvenile fiction. 4. Galveston (Tex.)—History—20th
century—Juvenile fiction. I. Title. II. Title: City of the dead.
PZ7.A5516Ch 2013
[Fic]—dc23   2012024491

Printed in China
(hc) 10 9 8 7 6 5 4 3 2 1

Display type set in Cracked and text type set in Adobe Caslon Pro
Printed and bound February 2013 by Jade Productions
in Heyuan, Guangdong, China

TABLE OF CONTENTS

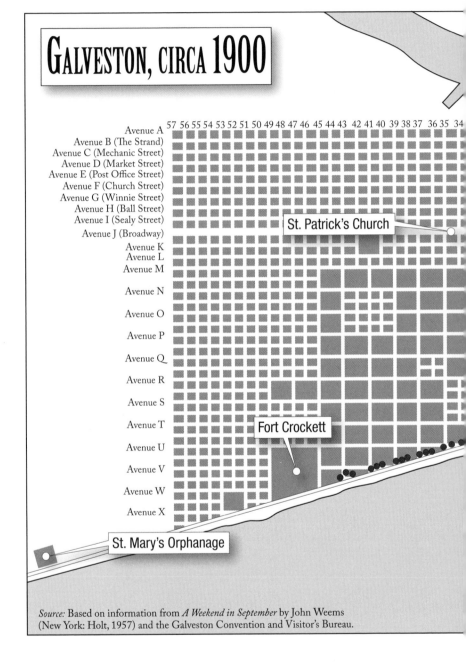

GALVESTON, CIRCA 1900

Avenue A
Avenue B (The Strand)
Avenue C (Mechanic Street)
Avenue D (Market Street)
Avenue E (Post Office Street)
Avenue F (Church Street)
Avenue G (Winnie Street)
Avenue H (Ball Street)
Avenue I (Sealy Street)
Avenue J (Broadway)
Avenue K
Avenue L
Avenue M
Avenue N
Avenue O
Avenue P
Avenue Q
Avenue R
Avenue S
Avenue T
Avenue U
Avenue V
Avenue W
Avenue X

57 56 55 54 53 52 51 50 49 48 47 46 45 44 43 42 41 40 39 38 37 36 35 34

St. Patrick's Church

Fort Crockett

St. Mary's Orphanage

Source: Based on information from *A Weekend in September* by John Weems (New York: Holt, 1957) and the Galveston Convention and Visitor's Bureau.

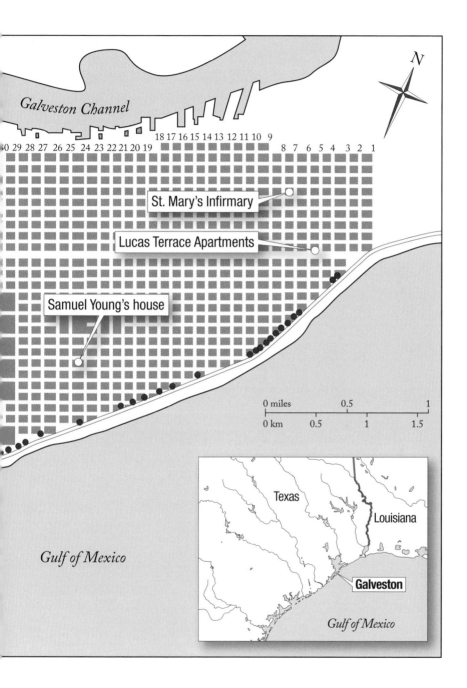

Galveston Channel

St. Mary's Infirmary

Lucas Terrace Apartments

Samuel Young's house

0 miles   0.5   1
0 km   0.5   1   1.5

Gulf of Mexico

Texas

Louisiana

Galveston

Gulf of Mexico

St. Louis, Mo., Sept. 9. The office of the Western Union Telegraph Company in this city is besieged with thousands of inquiries as to the extent and result of the terrible storm that cut off Galveston, Texas, from communication with the rest of the world. Rumors of the most direful nature come from that part of Texas, some of them even intimating that Galveston has been entirely wrecked and that the bay is covered with the dead bodies of its residents.

—Western Union, September 9, 1900

PROLOGUE

THE YOUNG NEWSPAPER REPORTER SAT in a small rowboat in Galveston Bay, not believing his eyes.

Human bodies bobbed facedown in the water, bumping against the boat. Men, women, children, babies. Swollen and lifeless. One corpse was twisted at the waist so that its face was visible, wide-eyed and stricken with terror.

The reporter had already spent five hours floating through the bay toward Galveston Island. Just three days before, Galveston, located three miles off the coast of Texas, had been shaken by a giant and brutal hurricane. As a gentle breeze nudged the boat through the calm water, the reporter now knew what he was moving toward: a city of the dead.

The sound of a rifle firing somewhere on the island sliced through the air as the boat reached the wharf.

This is what the end of the world looks like, the reporter thought. He staggered into a city that had been shaken to its foundation. As far as the eye could see, houses lay in ruins. He passed worn men grouped about the streets, speaking in hushed tones, their faces blank. Sad-eyed women picked over the remains of their demolished houses. Children with cuts on their faces, barely dressed in tattered clothing, sat on piles of wood.

Bodies lay in the rubble. Some were buried under piles of bricks. Some had sharp pieces of timber lodged in their head. Most had been stripped naked by the storm and thrown like rag dolls across the ground.

The reporter saw smoke rising from behind a long stretch of mangled houses up ahead on the other side of the narrow island. *What could have caught fire in this sodden place?* The smell of rotting flesh emanated from within the endless piles of timber and brick. The reporter pressed on, struggling to keep from being sick. He gripped his nose and mouth with his hand to block out the stench, stepping over cooking utensils, tablecloths, window frames, toys, candles, books, bicycles, and empty dresser drawers. Ahead of him he saw trees uprooted and driven through houses like nails through a board, telephone poles that had been lifted up and thrown like darts, a piano lodged in the window of a capsized house.

He finally reached the shore on the south side of the island. A scarred beach stretched before him, the sand blotched with refuse and splattered with blood. Here and there along the mutilated shore, pools of slimy water stank with the dead bodies of chickens, birds, horses, dogs, and cats. Ahead for what seemed like a mile, destroyed pieces of houses and machinery from midway games stuck out of the water. Down the beach a giant fire blazed, fed with the timbers of wrecked homes.

The reporter stood on the beach and watched men pull bodies from the sand. One man in particular stood out, because he was struggling to lift the tiny body of a very young boy. Something was keeping the body buried in the ground.

The man knelt down and started scooping sand from around the body. Seeing a length of clothesline around the boy's waist, he pulled on the line. Yet another body emerged from under the sand—a girl's this time, also with clothesline tied around her waist. The man followed the line and continued pulling. Another child's body surfaced, also a young girl. With tears in his eyes, the man continued pulling and digging. A boy appeared, holding the hand of another boy. More pulling on the line. A girl surfaced next, the fingers of one hand gripping the clothesline. After more digging, the man unearthed two more girls, locked in a horrified embrace, the head of one of them nestled into the chest of the other, their wet hair intertwined. Then a final grim tug, and a boy with a gash in his head came into view.

Nine children, tied together. All dead.

Through his tears the man saw that the boy with the head wound was holding on to something not yet visible beneath the sand. Trembling, the man pulled once again on the line.

It was the body of a nun. Her eyes were open, gazing up at the heavens.

The reporter couldn't watch any longer. He turned his head and looked down the beach. What was that he could see men dragging from the shore and over to the fire?

Bodies and more bodies. Now in heaps by the hundreds. Swollen and soaked. Decomposed. Waiting to feed the flames.

On September 7, 1900, Galveston, Texas, was a thriving island city of thirty-eight thousand people. It was a busy port with many oceangoing vessels at anchor, a travel destination connected to the Texas mainland by a railway bridge. A popular beach resort, the city was bursting with natural beauty—roses, oleanders, palm trees—as well as the finest shops and handsomest man-made structures that the Gilded Age could offer.

By September 9, Galveston was a city utterly destroyed, victim of the worst natural disaster in American history. An estimated eight thousand people were dead, and many thousands were homeless. Galveston was a waterlogged wreck, its bridge to the mainland wiped out, its communications with the rest of the country cut. Beaches, buildings, ships, houses—all were cemeteries hiding their dead in unmarked graves.

The storm had no name. It arrived on the morning of September 8, 1900, with whipping winds and rising water. By noon it was banging ferociously on Galveston's door. . . .

WAVES BREAKING

AT 7:00 A.M. ON SATURDAY, September 8, rain pelted the streets of downtown Galveston as a horse-drawn wagon came to a halt in front of St. Mary's Infirmary. St. Mary's, a hospital on Market Street in the northeast part of Galveston, sat six blocks west of the beach. Seawater had already broken free of the shoreline and begun to crawl up the streets.

"More Galveston overflow, huh, Henry?" Sister Elizabeth Ryan said to the driver, Henry Esquior. Sister Ryan opened the wagon door, looked up into the darkening sky, and stepped out with an umbrella. Much as she hated venturing out in this downpour, the food for St. Mary's Orphanage, run by the Sisters of Charity, had to be picked up. The Sisters had barely had enough provisions in the pantry to give the children a proper breakfast that morning.

"Yes, ma'am. The water is moving faster than usual, though, ain't it?" he replied. Henry leaned over to pat his horse on the backside. The horse shook its head irritably.

"Hmmm, I suppose so. . . . Well, we'll be as quick as we can. Come along, boys!" Sister Elizabeth reached out to assist two boys out of the wagon, but the boys had already hopped out of the other side and circled around to stand quietly behind Sister Elizabeth. Turning around, Sister Elizabeth jumped when she saw the smiling faces of William Murney and James Whitaker, both thirteen, and she dropped the umbrella on the street. The boys erupted with laughter.

"Boys! You just about scared the life out of me," she scolded. By way of apology, James, the taller of the two, picked up the umbrella, reached to hold it over Sister Elizabeth's head, and offered her his hand. They made their way to the back entrance of the infirmary, the water washing over their boots as they walked.

"Rain on a Saturday," William said with disappointment. He looked over at James, who nodded and wiped droplets of rain off of his nose.

"Maybe it'll stop later," James said. "Sister Elizabeth, if the rain lets up can we still play ball by the dunes?"

Sister Elizabeth looked at the water collecting in the street. "I don't think this rain is going away any time soon, love. Look at that sky!"

James and William stepped out from under the umbrella. They lifted their faces to the threatening sky but dropped them quickly, bristling at the pain of the lashing raindrops in their eyes.

Noting the boys' disappointment, Sister Elizabeth said, "We'll see how it looks when we get back to the orphanage. First things first—we need to see Mother Gabriel and get the boxes of food she's prepared for us. We'll worry about playtime later."

They arrived at the back door and Sister Elizabeth held it open. "In you go," she said.

———◦◦◦———

Daisy Thorne woke up to the sound of the wind and rain rattling her window. She got out of bed and padded to the window of her room, which was on the second floor of the Lucas Terrace apartment building, five blocks south of Saint Mary's Infirmary. She saw water ebbing in from the Gulf as it usually did during overflows like this, flooding the section of Broadway where her building stood. She sighed.

Not another rainy Saturday, she thought. Then she remembered what she had bought yesterday. Her face brightened, and she bounded down the staircase to the first floor. She grabbed the family's new Kodak Brownie camera from its place on the mantel. She had bought it with money saved from her job teaching seventh grade at the Rosenberg School. Though she had felt a little guilty for spending so much money all at once—she was usually so frugal—Daisy was now excited to have the camera, having bought it just in time for the biggest storm of the season so far.

"Daisy?" her mother said from the kitchen. "What are you doing?"

Daisy stopped at the front door and turned back. "Good morning, Mother," she said, popping her head into the kitchen. She smiled at her mother and her aunt Clara, who sat next to her. "Good morning, Auntie. Just want to get some photos of the water!"

Before her mother had a chance to say no, Daisy turned and hurried back to the front door.

"Well, be careful with that camera!" her mother shouted after her.

On the porch Daisy went to the bottom of the stairs. The water was swirling just below. She saw families walking past her building toward the beach to watch the giant waves rolling in and pushing water into town.

Daisy called out to her neighbor Mrs. Hesse, whom she saw walking with her husband and twelve-year-old son, Vernon. They were all dressed in black raincoats, and Mr. Hesse held a large umbrella over his and his wife's heads. Young Vernon rushed ahead, impatient to get to the beach.

"Good morning, Mrs. Hesse!" Daisy shouted. "Let me know how big the waves are!"

Mrs. Hesse waved to Daisy and continued on, scuttling to try to keep up with Vernon. For a moment Daisy considered throwing her raincoat and galoshes on and joining the Hesses but decided against it—at twenty-three, she was a little too old to splash around in the rain. Her mother would have a fit. And besides, Daisy really wanted to see what her brand-new Kodak could do.

Stepping back up to the porch, Daisy took pictures of the water rolling in from the beach, undaunted by the rising tide. Some of her happiest memories from her childhood, after all, were those times when she had splashed and played in the overflow of water from the Gulf with her little brother Bradley and their father. Daisy bit her lip as she remembered her daddy lifting her out of the water and pretending that he was a sea monster carrying her away to his lair as she screamed and giggled. It was hard to believe he was dead five years already.

Daisy saw two young boys riding the water past Lucas Terrace on a sheet of wood, laughing. Lifting her camera, she tried to get a shot of them as they sailed along. Just as she clicked the shutter, the boys' vessel slammed into the base of a nearby tree, and they tumbled off and into the water, now about a foot deep.

"Are you boys OK?" Daisy yelled after them.

The boys stood up and looked at the piece of wood, still lodged against the tree thanks to the continually flowing water. They looked over at Daisy, laughed, grabbed the wood, and ran through the running water back toward the beach.

On the south side of Galveston Island, Dr. Samuel Young stood on the beach facing the Gulf of Mexico. He lived close by, just four blocks inland. An amateur weather forecaster, Sam frowned at the high level of the tide.

He watched as the rising water lapped at the streetcar trestle that ran along the beach. The rain was really falling now, and the increasing wind was coming from the north. Normally, when the wind came from the north the tide would be low. So low, in fact, that, as an acquaintance of Sam's often joked, "You could walk halfway to Cuba." So why was the tide so terribly high this time?

Sam already knew the answer, for he had been noticing unusual weather patterns for a few days now. On Wednesday, for example, the tide was high and the water was rough, but there was no wind blowing to explain these occurrences. The air was completely still, which suggested that something in the Gulf must be pushing the water in. Thursday was the same— high tide, rough water, but no wind. One thing that was different today, though, was the haziness of the atmosphere. A haziness, Sam knew, that usually preceded a serious storm.

A cyclone is coming, Sam thought. And it had to be a

powerful one, if the tide was rising this quickly. He couldn't help feeling some excitement at the prospect of another great storm moving through town. He knew it would be a headache to deal with tomorrow, but Galveston during a storm was a spectacular sight.

He continued watching the waves—what Galvestonians called "rollers"—come in for a few minutes, then gazed way out to where the sea met the sky, squinting his eyes in a useless effort to bring the scene into focus. After a few minutes, he looked again at the streetcar trestle. The water was now breaking over it.

Sam walked away from the beach. His wife and children were headed for Galveston on a train from the west. He resolved to go downtown to the Western Union telegraph office and wire a message to be delivered to them when their train stopped at the station in San Antonio. He didn't want them trying to reach Galveston in this mess.

Sam started composing the telegram in his head: *My Dearest Maud. Great storm upon us. Go no farther on this train. I'll meet you in San Antonio. No need to worry the children or feel anxious about me. Will send for you. With love, Sam.*

———◦◦◦———

At St. Mary's Infirmary, Mother Gabriel handed a box of supplies to William to take out to the wagon.

"Careful, child, it's heavy."

William gripped the box tightly with both hands and pushed down on the top of it with his chin. He walked clumsily to the door, which Sister Elizabeth held open for him. She

Portrait of William Murney, circa 1900

smiled as he carefully stepped down onto the pavement, now covered with rushing water. Outside James stood by the wagon, packing boxes into the back. He saw William and helped him put the last box in place.

"Sister Elizabeth," Mother Gabriel said, "I do wish you and the boys would stay until the storm has passed. It's dreadfully wet out and the rain doesn't appear to be letting up. You'll be safer here."

Sister Elizabeth shook her head. "Oh, Mother Gabriel, I just couldn't. If the boys and I don't make it back, the children won't have any supper. Our cupboards are quite bare."

She opened the back door and saw William and James playing in the rain. They were taking turns jumping up and down and seeing who could produce the biggest splash.

"Boys!" Sister Elizabeth yelled out the door. William and James froze, arms by their sides, and struggled not to laugh. Elizabeth turned back to Mother Gabriel.

"We'll be fine, Reverend Mother, really."

Mother Gabriel gazed out the window at the gray sky and steady rain. "Well, all right. I wouldn't want the children to go hungry. But do take care on your way back, won't you? It's such a long drive to the orphanage."

"Yes, of course. Thank you, Mother Gabriel. I'll telephone when we get back."

"Very well, Sister Elizabeth. God be with you, my dear."

"And with you, Reverend Mother."

Sister Elizabeth opened the door and stepped back out into the rain. It seemed as if the water had risen at least a few inches just since their arrival at the hospital.

"Boys, into the wagon, please. Come along," Sister Elizabeth said. William and James stopped their splashing game and obediently seated themselves in the vehicle. Sister Elizabeth climbed in next to them.

"OK, Henry, sorry for the wait. We're ready," she said.

Henry nodded and shook the reins, stirring the horse into action. "Come on, girl, let's get on home," he said.

———•◆•———

Upstairs at the rain-pummeled Lucas Terrace, Daisy traced her fingers along a bookshelf in her mother's bedroom. At last she found the title she was looking for: *The Love Letters of Robert Browning and Elizabeth Barrett Browning*. She opened the cover to read the handwritten message inside:

> *To my dearest Daisy, with much love,*
> *Joe*

Blushing, Daisy closed the book, tucked it under her arm. After poking her head out of the door to make sure the coast was clear, she ducked back to her bedroom.

Of course, her mother knew about Joe. He was Daisy's fiancé, after all. But Daisy still didn't want to get caught by her mother or her aunt—or, God forbid, her brother!—reading a book of love letters given to her by the man she would marry next June.

Daisy brought the book into her bedroom and closed the door. She walked to the window and gazed outside. The water was still coming in from the beach, and the level was quickly rising above the curbs and flowing into the yard. Soaking wet families were rushing back from their short beach trips, obviously having seen enough big waves to last them a while. Daisy saw someone exit the Hesse house across the street; it was their teenage daughter, Irene. Irene stood outside looking worriedly at the water swirling around her ankles, then took off running down Broadway, away from the beach.

Daisy watched as the boys on the makeshift raft glided by again this time much more quickly, successfully averting the tree that had halted their joyride the last time. A few minutes later, Daisy saw Mr. and Mrs. Hesse once again chasing after their son, Vernon. He was in as much of a rush to get home and dry as he had been to get to the beach a half hour earlier.

Daisy turned from the window and sat down in the chair in the corner of her room. *What a mess*, she thought, opening the book of love letters. It was a good day to just stay in and read.

After sending the telegram to his wife, Sam Young stood at the wharf looking out over Galveston Bay on the north side of the island. He had walked there to see how things looked on this side before walking south and returning home. He wasn't too worried about his house. He'd seen it withstand worse storms than this one appeared to be. There would be water damage, no doubt, but nothing too terrible. The beach, though, and the buildings sitting on it, would probably need some repairs tomorrow.

The wind must be more than fifty miles per hour, he thought. The water was now over the wharves and flowing inland. Sam began his walk south toward his house eighteen blocks away. It would be a long walk, and a messy one. The water flowed around his feet.

He walked as quickly as he could, increasingly curious about what was happening on the Gulf side of the island. Soon he reached the Strand, a normally bustling downtown street with shops and restaurants that served the city's well-to-do. The water from the bay had already risen above the curbs. The rain was now a downpour. By the Tremont Hotel, Sam saw workmen in overalls and caps standing on ladders. As the rain got harder, they climbed down to street level to seek shelter. Shoppers stood behind glass doors in the store entryways, watching the rain pelt down and the water creep closer and closer.

Sam kept walking. It wasn't until he reached Galveston's center, at the middle part of Avenue K, that his feet were no longer under water. He ran through the driving rain and whipping wind, finally reaching the south shore. The tide had covered the beach and advanced up the streets.

Sam gazed out toward the Gulf. He was shocked to see that the railway trestle was now twisted and gnarled up by the wind and waves. He looked over at another familiar landmark, the Pagoda bathhouse, which stood in front of the Beach Hotel on Twenty-fourth Street. The water was quickly overtaking it. The wind whipped against the bathhouse with increasing fury, peeling off pieces of timber and hurling them into the air.

Sam shivered and turned around. He sloshed down Twenty-fourth Street five blocks to his house on P½ Street. When he got there he saw the house surrounded by two feet of water. Still, his lot was raised four feet off the ground as a precaution against these Galveston overflows. The water line could go even two feet higher and still his first floor would not be touched.

Sam decided to sit on his porch and enjoy the view of this, the most exciting show he'd seen in some time. He'd waded into it and seen the excitement in other parts of town. Now he just wanted to sit back and watch.

Meanwhile, the water crept ever closer toward his porch steps.

Three miles west of Sam Young's house, a small group of

St. Mary's Orphanage, circa 1900

boys splashed around in front of their dormitory at St. Mary's Orphanage. The orphanage's two large two-story buildings sat just off the beach behind a row of tall sand dunes supported by salt cedar trees.

The water was up to the boys' shins, and they competed to see who could kick a spray of water the farthest. One of the boys, twelve-year-old Frank Madera, managed to scatter drops of water as far as fifteen feet. The others cheered for him as he walked back to the porch steps to sit down. He noticed that the water had risen up to the first step already.

"Wow, look!" he said. The other boys turned back and stared at the water lapping hungrily at the bottom of the wooden step. Then they went back to their game; there were plenty more waves to kick.

Another boy, Albert Campbell, twelve years old, stood alone at the corner of the building, his feet submerged in a foot of water. He alternated his gaze between the group of boys play-ing and the large waves coming in from the Gulf. A few minutes before, he had been kicking waves along with the others. But then he had fallen down, face-first, into the water. The shock of water going into his open mouth spooked him, and he moved away from the group as they continued to play.

He wondered how his sister Maggie was doing in the girls' dormitory next door. She was two years younger, and she scared easily. Ever since their parents died and their older sister, Mary Ann, had placed them at the orphanage temporarily, Albert had been determined to protect her. In a few months, they would be able to join Mary Ann and her husband at their new home in Topeka, Kansas. Until then, he saw looking after Maggie as his most important duty.

"Boys, that's quite enough!" called Sister Camillus Tracy, bounding out the porch door. She stood at the top of the stairs and clapped her hands as the boys, shouting and pushing and falling over, continued to play.

"*Boys!*"

They turned to face Sister Camillus. As the oldest of the group, Frank was the assumed spokesman. "We're sorry, Sister Camillus," he shouted over the roar of the wind and the crashing of the large waves in the distance. "We were gonna play ball, but . . ." He looked down at his feet, which were barely visible beneath the salty Gulf water.

Sister Camillus nodded and smiled. "But you decided that it would be more fun to splash around and soak yourselves to the bone!"

Frank smiled back at Sister Camillus. She always liked to give him a hard time.

"Inside, all of you," she commanded them. "Come along! Get some dry clothes on."

The boys moved up the steps. Sister Camillus remained on the porch until all of them were inside. She looked around at the yard and the swirling water, and she realized something.

"Wasn't Albert out here?" She called out to him. "Albert? Albert!"

But Albert was gone.

SEEKING SHELTER

A DRENCHED FIGURE POUNDED ON Sam Young's back door with
wet knuckles.

It was Charlie, the young black man who worked on Sam's
lawn every Saturday morning. He'd come early today, hoping
to cut the grass in the backyard, trim the hedges, and get a
little work done on the cobbled footpath before the rain got
too bad. A native Galvestonian, Charlie was used to working in
the rain, especially in September and October, when Galveston
had plenty of soggy days.

But this morning's relentless downpour kept him from getting much of anything done. He'd spent the last hour on the
back porch watching the water rise, feeling the wind rip, and trying to think of ways to stay and get more work done—he hated
to leave and give up a day's pay. Was there anything Dr. Young
needed doing *inside* the house?

Charlie knocked again on the back door. After waiting a few
minutes for Dr. Young to answer, Charlie looked around warily
to see if anyone was around, then tried turning the doorknob to

see if it was unlocked. Maybe Dr. Young was inside and unable to hear him knocking over the sound of the rain. No, the door was locked. Charlie was going to have to accept that he would get no work done today. He stepped off the covered back porch and, with a splash, landed on the unfinished cobbled path he had started constructing just last week.

The water was up to his shins. He sloshed through the water and around the house to the front porch, where, to his surprise, he saw Dr. Young sitting in one of the rocking chairs and calmly looking out at the incoming tide.

"Dr. Young? Think I won't be able to do any work on the yard today, sir."

Sam looked over at Charlie and laughed.

"Charlie! Get out of that rain, friend!" Sam said, standing up on his front porch. "Come on up here!"

Charlie smiled. "Thank you, sir!"

"It's a nasty storm coming," Sam said as he helped the young man up the submerged steps. "I think it could do some real damage."

"As long as it doesn't mess too much with the work I've done on your toolshed, Dr. Young, this storm can do what it wants!"

"Oh, she will, Charlie, mark my words." Sam smiled and lightly slapped Charlie on the back. "That toolshed is likely to start floating any minute now."

A spray of water hit Sam and Charlie in their faces, shocking them into silence. The water had reached the top step.

"What say you follow me inside and help me board up these pesky windows while we've still got light? The electricity is sure to go out soon, and this wind is getting awfully angry." Sam looked at the sky.

St. Mary's Orphanage Chapel, circa 1900

"Not terribly worried about the water creeping into the house," he continued, "but I daresay I'm spooked by the speed of this overflow."

Charlie smiled, relieved that there was at least some work to be done. "I'm happy to come in and help, Dr. Young."

"Very well, then, after you," Sam said. He held the front door open for Charlie, and the two men went inside as the water flowed over the edge of the porch.

———◦◦◦———

Albert trudged up the steps of the new girls' dormitory, searching for Maggie. Both dormitories, which stood side by side behind a dense thicket of salt cedar trees, were now surrounded by three feet of water. Behind him he heard shouting and playful shrieking over at the boys' building. But Albert could hear no such commotion coming from the girls' building. The only noise came from the moaning wind and the rain beating against the building.

"Maggie!"

Albert swung open the screen door and hopped inside. There were no lights on, and he could see no signs of anyone in the large sitting room by the entrance or in the nearby kitchen. Walking down the long hallway, all he could hear was the wind whipping around outside. But as he continued to the end of the hall, he began to hear muffled voices over the wind. There was singing coming from the chapel. He leaned in close to the chapel door and put his ear against it, listening to the strains of a familiar hymn:

> *See how the waters with tumultuous motion*
> *Rise up and foam without a pause or rest.*
> *But fear we not, tho' storm clouds round us gather,*
> *Thou art our Mother and thy little Child*
> *Is the All Merciful, our loving Brother*
> *God of the sea and of the tempest wild.*

It was "Queen of the Waves," a song the nuns always sang with the children during storms. The girls must be upset.

Albert opened the chapel door as quietly as he could and scanned the room for Maggie. Mother Camillus Tracy stood at the front of the chapel, leading the singing. Dozens of girls clustered together in the pews, their backs to Albert. They calmly nodded their heads as Mother Camillus directed them with her hands.

Maggie was all alone in the last pew, wearing a white summer dress. She sat with her knees bent and her heels on the edge of the pew. Her arms were wrapped around her legs and she looked scared.

"Is that young Albert?" Mother Camillus said, dropping her hands by her side, interrupting the singing. All of the girls turned their heads toward the back of the chapel. The wind and rain pummeled the walls around them. Maggie turned and saw Albert. Her face brightened.

His face flushing, Albert stumbled through the door. "Yes, ma'am. . . . Sorry, I just wanted to check on Maggie."

"Well, come in, child. But only if you sing with us!"

Albert shuffled over to where Maggie sat and joined her in the pew. She was smiling but she couldn't hide her fear—her hands were clasped together, shaking slightly.

"Maggie, it's OK, it's just a storm." Albert took one of her hands in his. "It just seems worse because we're so close to the beach." This appeared to make sense to Maggie—she nodded and turned her attention back to Mother Camillus.

"OK, let's continue from the second stanza, shall we?" Mother Camillus said, raising her hands to direct the singing once again.

Albert and Maggie opened their mouths to sing, trying to ignore the increasingly violent wind pounding on the walls.

———•◦•———

A furious knocking at the door downstairs woke Daisy. She had been reading in the rocking chair in her bedroom and had fallen asleep with her cat Jasper on her lap and the book of poetry open facedown on her chest. Quickly tossing the book onto her bed and Jasper onto the floor, she rushed out of the room. She stopped at the parlor, where she was surprised to see a group of people had gathered and were talking in hushed tones. She recognized all of them from the neighborhood, and they were wet to the bone. There was Gus Amundsen, who lived a few apartments over, and Robert Lauderdale, whose apartment was at the very end of the building. Donald and Mary Morton and their young children, Lilly and Kyle, lived in a house across the street. Emma Sutton rented a room in a nearby house on Sixth Street.

Daisy hustled down the stairs to see who was knocking, but her mother was already opening the door. It was the Dawsons, who lived in the house next to Lucas Terrace on Broadway. Their shivering faces were white and dripping wet.

"Hello, do come in," Daisy's mother, Alice, said. "This storm is wretched!"

Daisy greeted the Dawsons and directed them up the stairs to join the others. "Mother, what has happened?"

"Oh, Daisy, it's dreadful," Alice said, closing the door. "Just dreadful. Everyone's house is flooding and they've come here for shelter."

This wasn't surprising. Lucas Terrace was a sturdy brick building, and Daisy's family's first-floor apartment was raised two feet above street level. Many of the houses nearby were much frailer wooden structures that flooded easily, though not usually enough to lead to so many wet guests.

"Well, we should get them some coffee and something to eat," Daisy said. "They all look like refugees!"

Daisy and Alice went into the kitchen, where her Aunt Talia was at the table, slicing bread. All five of her cats mewed on the floor in front of their food bowl. Daisy began preparing coffee, and her mother helped Talia make sandwiches. Soon there was another knock at the door.

Daisy opened the door to see Mr. and Mrs. Hesse standing there with their son, Vernon. They were all still clad in the raincoats she'd seen them in earlier.

"Daisy," Mrs. Hesse said, "could we stay here for a little while? Our house is just a wreck. The water is up to the top of the coffee table!"

"Oh, please come in, you poor things!" Daisy said. "Let me take your raincoats. There are a few other folks upstairs in the parlor. Mother is making sandwiches and coffee."

As Vernon and Mr. Hesse walked up the steps, Mrs. Hesse looked at Daisy and said in a hushed tone, "Honey, we're worried about Irene. We haven't seen her since this morning."

Daisy froze, remembering the image of Irene leaving the Hesse house and running down Broadway away from the beach earlier that morning. She had assumed that Irene would eventually get tired and return home. "She never came back?" Daisy said.

"Came back from *where*, Daisy?"

———◆———

Upstairs Sam and Charlie were almost finished securing the windows and doors. After nailing plywood to most of the windows, they went around and closed all the doors and leaned the chairs against the doorknobs. As Charlie began to roll out tape to fasten the doors to the walls, the lights went out.

"You better get home, Charlie," Sam said. "Make sure your family is OK."

Charlie nodded. "Sure enough. I'll let myself out, Dr. Young. See you next Saturday." Charlie walked downstairs, leaving Sam in the sitting room where the last of the windows waited to be boarded up.

In the front yard, the water had risen unbelievably fast—it was nearly to Charlie's waist as he waded down Twenty-third Street.

Upstairs, Sam wondered how Charlie would fair on his trip home through the rising water. Although it wasn't even two o'clock yet, with most of the windows now boarded up, the house was in darkness. He decided to go downstairs to get a candle out of the china cabinet in the living room.

He carefully descended the stairs, feeling around for each step with his feet before stepping down. But as he approached the bottom he saw a sight, illuminated by the light coming through the transom, that sent a shiver up his spine: the water was up to the first step. Inside the house. The four-foot brick pillars his house stood on had not saved the interior from the rising water. They had only delayed the surge.

He stepped down to the floor and found himself in water up to his ankles. Gazing into the living room, he saw water licking the legs of the couch and coffee table.

Sam couldn't believe it—he'd been sure that he would be able to just sit and watch the storm from the safety of his house without having to worry about it finding its way inside.

A small framed picture of the Young family, taken on the south shore of Galveston the previous summer, floated past him toward the vestibule.

———·◆·———

At the orphanage William Murney and James Whitaker stood on the porch, struggling to remain on their feet in the driving wind. They had finally made it back with Sister Elizabeth and Henry, hours after setting out from the St. Mary's Infirmary in the center of Galveston. The trip back to the orphanage had been treacherous: by the time they were halfway home, the wagon's wheels were slogging through two feet of water.

The boys had just taken the last box of supplies from the wagon inside but had snuck back out to test their strength against the wind, which was gusting at over thirty miles per hour. They had to admit, the wind was winning.

With unbelieving eyes William and James surveyed the scene in front of the dormitory. The tide was eroding the sand

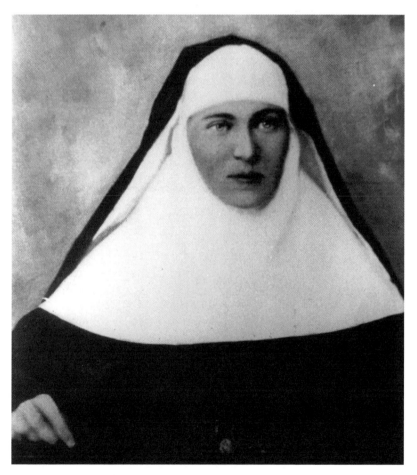

Portrait of Sister Elizabeth Ryan, circa 1890s

dunes as if they had been made of flour. Branches and pieces of roofing flew through the air. The wind shrieked and moaned, pushing William back against the building. Having had enough, he scurried back into the dormitory. James remained on the porch, leaning forward into the wind.

Inside, Sister Elizabeth and Sister Raphael were unpacking the groceries. "Oh, Sister Raphael, it was just terrible. Things were flying through the air and hitting the wagon! I thought we were done for, I honestly did."

"Well, you're here now, and safe," Sister Raphael said. "Mother Camillus has already taken the girls into the chapel to try to calm their nerves. Some of them seem ever so frightened—Oh my dear Lord, *William!*"

Sister Raphael jumped as she saw William dripping wet in the doorway of the kitchen. "What is it you need, dear boy?"

"I wonder if I could get a snack for Joseph." Joseph was William's little brother. William knew the Sisters had a soft spot for Joseph, who was only two when their parents died six years ago.

"Oh, very well," Sister Raphael said, taking two large crackers from a cookie tin she had just filled and handing them to William. "Make sure Joseph gets one of these," she said, smiling as William dashed out. "Oh, and William!"

William walked back into the kitchen.

"Where's James? Wasn't he with you?"

"He's still on the porch."

"Well, tell him to get inside. That's no place for him to be."

"Yes, ma'am."

William walked back to the porch door and looked outside, but James wasn't out there. He shrugged. James must have given up on fighting the wind and come inside.

William turned and walked down the main hallway to look for Joseph. A few minutes later, he found his brother huddling with a group of boys in the room of bunk beds they all shared. They were gathered around the window, watching the tempest outside. Joseph was enraptured, his face a mixture of awe and uncertainty. "It's OK, ol' Joe," Frank Madera said, sitting on a bed behind him. "You know these storms can be almighty, but they have to die down sometime."

"But the . . . ," Joseph began to say, but he couldn't find the words to describe what he was seeing. To him the wind seemed like an invisible monster, tearing through the salt cedar trees and spitting rain against the windowpanes.

"Joseph," William called from the doorway. Joseph looked over and William signaled for him to come out into the hallway. Joseph furrowed his brow and shook his head. William backed away from the door and, with a smile on his face, held out the crackers he had gotten from Sister Raphael.

Joseph came running. As he grabbed a cracker out of William's hand, the window in the room behind him shattered inward, spraying glass inside and over the boys. Joseph turned around and watched in horror from the hallway as the boys—who just moments ago sat and watched bravely as the wind and rain battered the window—now flailed away from it, screaming wildly.

A spray of blood dotted the room's hardwood floor. William yanked his baby brother out of the room as the wind slammed the door shut.

———·•◆•·———

In their Lucas Terrace apartment, Alice and Aunt Talia made more sandwiches by candlelight, and Daisy prepared fresh coffee.

"It's a good thing we stopped by the grocery store last night," Alice muttered. There were almost twenty people in the upstairs parlor now—they had all fled their houses when the flooding became too great. The increasingly shrill cries of the cats reverberated through the living room.

"I wonder how the McCauleys are doing next door," Daisy mused. "That poor man in the wheelchair. . . . Should I go try to check on them?"

"Yes," Alice replied. "We should do that. I'm sure Mrs. McCauley will need help. Why don't you go up and finish serving the coffee, then bring Danny downstairs, and you and he can go over there."

Coffeepot in hand, Daisy headed to the staircase. She stopped at the front door and peered out of the small side window, gawking at the ferocity outside. Debris flew through the air, and she could see trash cans and pieces of wood gliding through the high water.

Daisy's brother, Danny, came hopping down the stairs and into the foyer. "Wow! I just saw part of a bathhouse fly by!" He pointed to the floor in front of the door. "Look, Daisy!"

Daisy gasped and stepped back. Water was quickly trickling into the apartment. She hurried to the linen closet for towels to stem the flow of water coming in. Determined not to panic, Daisy turned to Danny and said in the stern tone she sometimes had to use with her students, "Now don't you go telling anybody about this, do you hear me?" Danny nodded with disappointment and shuffled off to the kitchen.

Daisy headed up the stairs to take care of their wet guests, trying to ignore the shrieks of Jasper and the other cats downstairs. Without giving away the dread growing inside her, she walked through the candlelit parlor, pouring coffee and offering words of comfort. As she approached the Hesses, she felt a pang of guilt. Even though Daisy knew that there was nothing she could have done to stop Irene from leaving the Hesse house earlier, she wished she had at least tried to do *something*. And she felt that Mrs. Hesse wished Daisy had done something, too.

"Please, have some more coffee," Daisy said, offering the pot.

"No, thank you," Mrs. Hesse said.

Daisy paused. "I'm sure she's fine, Mrs. Hesse. She probably ran to a friend's house farther inland. You know she always hated these storms."

Mrs. Hesse nodded, but her face was wrinkled with fear.

Daisy placed a hand on Mrs. Hesse's shoulder and lingered for a moment longer, then continued circulating with the coffee, speaking quietly with the Dawsons; checking in on Gus and Robert; making sure that Emma was warm enough; and trying to console the frightened Morton children, who huddled with their parents in the corner. At the parlor window, which looked out over Broadway, she marveled at the water rushing along the street, thinking it must be what river rapids look like. She was about to go downstairs for the sandwiches, when out of the corner of her eye she saw something outside that was so incredible, it took a second for her brain to understand it.

The water had lifted up an entire house and swept it down the street like an upset toddler angrily hurling a toy in the bathtub. It was the Hesses' house.

Daisy turned to Mrs. Hesse and opened her mouth, but

then realized she had no idea what to say. Instead she looked back out the window, just in time to see the wind crumple up the house and hurl it into the tide like a piece of paper.

———◦◦◦———

The Gulf of Mexico surrounded the dormitories at St. Mary's Orphanage. Only the longest and highest branches of the salt cedar trees in front of the buildings were still above the waterline.

Something floated by a cluster of trees and became caught in the branches of one of them. It was the lifeless body of a young boy, floating facedown. The thrusts of the wind rolled the body over and over, eventually pinning it against one of the branches.

It was James Whitaker.

COLLAPSE

GALVESTON WAS DISAPPEARING. THE HURRICANE winds charged in from the Gulf of Mexico, pushing the tide farther into town, where the Gulf water converged with water from Galveston Bay, driven by a violent wind from the north. The entire city would soon be under water.

Shortly after 6 p.m., the Celtic cross atop Saint Patrick's Church, the tallest structure in the city, crashed to earth. Although he was struggling down Twenty-third Street only eleven blocks away, Charlie couldn't hear the crash over the roaring wind.

After saying good-bye to Sam Young, Charlie waded as quickly as he could down Twenty-third Street toward his house. He fought to stay on his feet against the whipping wind and the water swirling around his waist. Pieces of houses flew past him, some flying in the wind, some sailing on the water. He heard people screaming.

He turned on Avenue N, toward his family's house on Twenty-seventh Street. A flailing woman sailing past grabbed him by the leg, digging her fingers into him and dragging him under the water as the tide pulled her along. Charlie wriggled free of her and leaped up, grabbing onto a tree. He watched with a mixture of relief and remorse as the woman sailed away on the tide, her face white with terror.

Still dizzy from his fall, Charlie climbed the tree. It was the only thing that would keep him from either flying into oblivion or being knocked down into the water again. He swung his leg around one of the branches and clung to it as the wind tried to peel him off.

As he held on, the tree swayed more and more violently. Charlie realized the roots of the tree were losing their grip on the earth.

Five blocks from Galveston's southern shore, Sam stood on the first floor of his house, which was submerged in two feet of water. Possessions that used to rest on the hardwood floor—a magazine rack, a piano stool, an end table—now bobbed on the water and floated around the room.

Sam was not prepared for this. Even though he had been watching the rising water all day and marveled at the relentless downpour of rain, still he had felt sure that the storm would end before invading his own house. He'd seen so many of these Gulf tempests over the years. Even the most ferocious always exhausted their anger before inviting themselves in. What was so different about this one?

A giant crashing sound sliced through the air outside. Sam waded toward the stairs. He needed to see what was going on outside, but he didn't dare open his front door. Instead he scaled the dark staircase calmly and walked into the second-floor sitting

Downtown Galveston before the storm

room. He pulled back the curtain at one of the few windows that he and Charlie hadn't managed to board up before the lights went out.

The street below was a fantastic sight. Boxes, barrels, carriages, cisterns, outhouses, pieces of timber, and small shacks glided past on the water. He could hear screaming. But he couldn't see anyone. He looked closely to try to discover human movement, but there was nothing, just objects sailing by. He stood up and went to get the hammer and nails he had left on the bureau, and when he returned to the window he caught a glimpse of something floating in his front yard.

A hand emerged into view, then an outstretched arm. Then the whole body. Lifeless, floating facedown. It was a young man, maybe eighteen years old, in tattered overalls flecked with streaks of white paint. His other arm was twisted behind him and his shoes had been torn from his feet.

Nails slid from Sam's slackening fingers and clinked to the floor.

— + ◆ + —

At Lucas Terrace the sound of yowling cats filled the first floor, where Alice and Aunt Talia were hunting in the dark for towels and blankets for their guests up in the parlor. The sudden crash of the Hesse house startled the cats into silence. Alice paused, her face briefly registering awareness of a nearby catastrophe before she resolved not to think about it. "Well, *something* shut the cats up, at least. Come along, Talia, these towels won't go upstairs themselves."

"But what about my little darlings?" Talia asked, stopping to look in on the cats in the living room.

"We'll come back for them later, dear," Alice said. "Or maybe Danny can bring them up. First things first."

Arms full and ankle deep in water, they made their way to the stairs, ignoring the cries of the cats in the living room. Alice stepped up and saw Daisy rushing down.

"Daisy, what on earth . . . ?" Alice said.

"Mother, it's awful, the Hesse house just . . . collapsed," Daisy said, speaking quickly in a forceful whisper.

Aunt Talia covered her mouth with her hands, dropping the towels.

"Talia, for heaven's sake!" Alice put her own towels on the stairs and reached out to rescue Talia's linens, floating in the water. "Well, I suppose someone should talk to them," she said.

"Mother, we can't tell them, now don't you dare!" Daisy

insisted, still whispering. "We've got to try to keep everyone as calm as possible, and Mrs. Hesse is already well nigh hysterical over Irene."

"Oh my lord," Talia said, "what if Irene was in the house when it . . . ?"

Daisy looked at Talia, quickly recognizing that this was, indeed, a possibility.

"There's nothing we can do about that now," Daisy said. "We've got to try to just take care of what we can. Auntie, dear, you and Mother get those blankets upstairs, and I'm going to look for more candles."

As Alice and Aunt Talia ascended the stairs, Daisy waded over to the front door, which was groaning from the pressure of the wind and water trying to beat their way in. She then recalled the one rule about storms that all Galvestonians know: once the rising water starts pushing against the house, it is important to relieve the external pressure on the building by either open-ing a door or drilling holes in the floor to allow some of the water in. Not having a drill in the apartment, Daisy decided her only option was to try to gradually let some water in through the door.

She slowly gripped the doorknob with both hands, leaning against the door to press against the surge.

"What are you doing?" her brother Danny yelped as he hopped down the stairs behind her. Daisy jumped and whipped around.

"Danny! Can't you do anything quietly? I'm going to let some of this water in."

"But won't the . . ." Before Danny could finish, Daisy cracked open the door and the Gulf exploded into the apartment, tossing Daisy and Danny into the back wall.

———◦◦◦———

In the boys' dormitory at the orphanage, Frank sat up and looked around to see if everyone was OK.

"Nick! Shep! You all right? Tony?" Frank looked around. A tree branch had flown through the window and fallen on Joseph's bed.

Slowly all the boys sat up, only one of them with a visible injury.

"Tony! Careful, stay still," Frank said. "You're bleeding."

Tony started to cry.

"It's OK, Tony, ol' boy!" Frank reassured him. "Just be still and let me. . . ."

Frank yanked a few shards of glass the size of fingernails out of Tony's cheek and forehead and wiped away other shards that had just scraped the skin.

"Ah . . . *ow*!" Tony shrieked. As blood flowed from the wounds, Frank grabbed a pillow from the closest bed and pressed it to Tony's face to stem the flow of blood.

In the hall William held Joseph's hand as more windows shattered. The crackers William had brought were now in pieces on the floor. The wind shot through the windows, bringing in rain, sand, and branches from the salt cedars.

"Boys! Boys! Come along!" Sister Raphael strode down the hallway, ringing a bell. Other sisters appeared, knocking on doors. "We must go over to the girls' dormitory immediately!"

The girls' dormitory was the newer and stronger of the two buildings. Every child at the orphanage knew that the chapel on the far end, where many of the girls had already gathered, had been designated by the Sisters as the safest place to be during a storm.

Water poured into the boys' building and more windows shattered. The sheltered walkway connecting the boys' dormitory to the girls' was now under water, and the cover was gone. The nuns herded the boys out the front door. Sister Elizabeth shouted over the screeching of the wind, "Listen, boys! Let's make a chain—everyone take the hand of the person nearest you. We've got to step down into the water just for a little while until we get to the other building. Everyone walk with your heads down!"

The boys descended the steps into the water. Frank walked with his arm around Tony, still clutching the bloody pillow. At the end of the line, William stepped down but was jerked back by Joseph, who had stopped at the top of the stairs.

"Come on, baby brother, let's go!" Joseph shook his head. "Joseph, we've got to go! The water isn't going to hurt you! We can walk through it! It's not very deep, you've done this before!"

Joseph was frozen with fear. As the turbulent water encircled the building, the dormitory was like a boat lost at sea.

"Little Joe," Sister Elizabeth said, running up behind him. "We must go! You'll be fine! I'll be right behind you!"

"Look!" William stepped down until he was in up to his thighs, then hopped back up. "It's easy as pie!" William pulled on Joseph's hand to coax him down. Joseph relented and took a step, then another step, and then another. As he reached the bottom, Sister Elizabeth grabbed his hand and swung him out and away from the porch.

As the wind increased in speed and the water continued its surge, fifty-four boys and five nuns waded across the divide between the two buildings, hands clasped together.

The dormitory shook.

———•◆•———

Sam saw dozens of bodies float past his house within a few minutes. After seeing that first dead body, he had moved to another window to look at a neighbor's fence that he'd been using to keep track of the water level. All of a sudden the wind changed direction from due west to due east, increasing in violence. As he watched, the water line on the fence rose about four feet in as many seconds.

Sam's house was pelted and sometimes punctured by flying debris. Two houses on the south side of P½ Street, between Twenty-fifth and Twenty-sixth, collapsed and floated away. His head swirling, Sam realized that this storm was no longer a show he could watch from the safety of his window. It was an attack that he would eventually—inevitably—have to fight against.

He sat in the gathering darkness thinking of his wife and children, who he hoped had stopped in San Antonio. Maybe they were enjoying a hot dinner at a hotel restaurant somewhere. He smiled to think at how excited the children would be to have an extra day away from home—they did so love staying in hotels.

Sam fetched the one candle that he'd been able to find in the china cabinet. He lit it with a match, walked back over to the window, and sat down. But after a few minutes of watching the storm by candlelight, he realized he should probably save the candle in case he needed it later. The darkness was only beginning, after all. He had an entire night ahead of him. He blew out the candle, placed it on the windowsill, and sat on the edge of his chair, ready to leap up when the time came. He knew the time to fight was coming soon.

The cats' chorus of wailing continued on the first floor of the Thorne apartment. Daisy opened her eyes and saw Jasper standing on the mantel looking down at her with wide eyes. Then Jasper was joined on the mantel by Button and Lizzie, both yowling loudly over each other, while Arthur and Sherlock clung to the couch on the other side of the room.

"Danny! Danny!" Daisy picked herself up off the floor, where she'd landed after the water had surged through the front door. The water was up to her knees. She saw Danny stumbling to his feet nearby and reached out to him.

"Are you OK?" she asked.

Danny coughed and spat water. "Yeah, you?"

"Fine."

Danny rushed out of the room and up the stairs.

"Danny, not a word!" Daisy shouted after him, knowing full well he wouldn't be able to keep his mouth shut for long. Daisy stood at the center of the room, looking from one side to the other. She was surrounded by spooked cats, their wails and confused cries filling the apartment. Furniture had risen off the floor.

Daisy stepped gingerly toward the mantel and picked up Jasper, who immediately latched onto her shoulder with his claws, growling.

Daisy's eyes watered from the pain of Jasper's grip. Slowly she lifted him off of her and disengaged his claws from her skin, cradling him tightly in her arms.

"Oh, sweet Jasper, it's OK, it's OK," she said, smoothing his ruffled wet fur. Jasper hissed.

Keeping a tight grip on Jasper, Daisy carefully grabbed Button off the mantel as Arthur and Sherlock jumped from the now-floating couch to the top of the china cabinet. The two cats in her arms knocked heads and hissed at each other, struggling against Daisy's grip and clawing at her dress. Daisy sloshed to the stairs and ran up to the parlor, where she hurled them onto the Victorian leaf cabinet. All conversation in the crowded room stopped as the two shrieking cats flew in, landed on the cabinet top, and then slid onto the floor.

"I'm sorry," Daisy said with a smile that barely masked her pain. "The cats are . . . upset."

"Jasper! Button!" Aunt Talia shouted, bringing the room back to life. "Come here, darlings. . . ."

Bleeding from her neck, cheek, and arms, Daisy glared at Aunt Talia briefly, then turned and dashed back downstairs to continue her cat rescue.

The wind changed direction abruptly and roared.

"It's getting worse! It's getting worse!" In one corner Mrs. Hesse was in a fit of panic. Her body trembled and she was starting to pull at her hair with both hands. "What are we going to do? It's coming closer!" She began to slam her back repeatedly against the wall.

Mr. Hesse and Alice tried to calm her down as some of the guests looked at her with blank faces, others with annoyance. Jasper and Button, now prowling around under the cabinet, continued to howl as debris crashed against the house and the wind shook the walls.

Gus, Robert, and Emma, now standing together against the wall, all looked at Mrs. Hesse as if she were a wild animal. "She's going mad," Gus whispered to the others.

A few minutes later, Daisy returned with two yowling cats in her arms and one on her head. Still bleeding, her dress now slit at the arm, Daisy again tossed the cats onto the cabinet.

"Daisy, you're bleeding, darling," Alice said as she scurried over to her daughter, relieved at the opportunity to escape Mrs. Hesse's hysterics. "Let's go clean you up."

Daisy and her mother went to the washroom. As Alice cleaned Daisy's face and neck, Daisy struggled to speak.

"Mother, I have to tell you . . . there has been a rush of water into the living room. There's a lot of water down there now . . . a lot of water." Daisy's voice trembled and she was short of breath. "And it's rising. . . ."

Alice dabbed at Daisy's face with witch hazel, nodding solemnly.

"Well, then," Alice said, finishing up with Daisy's wounds, "we'll just have to make sure everyone stays upstairs, won't we?" Alice smiled with her eyes.

Daisy nodded vaguely. "Yes, I suppose so."

"Now, let me go back down to the kitchen to get some things. When you finish in here would you be a dear and go do your best to calm that Mrs. Hesse down?"

"Yes, Mother."

Alice touched Daisy's cheek, walked out of the washroom, and closed the door. Daisy looked in the mirror and fixed her hair, which Sherlock had disheveled mightily. She swirled it into a bun on top of her head, splashed her face with water, and walked out into the hall. But she didn't go back into the parlor. She walked straight past it and into her room, closing the door behind her. From her dresser she retrieved a small handbag, which contained twenty five-dollar pieces. She and Joe had planned on using the money to buy furniture for their home after their wedding. Now she stood there with the bag in her hand, knowing she better take it with her as she might not make it back to this room, after all.

She peered out her window. Every house on her street was gone.

Mother Camillus looked at Sister Raphael with a grave expression as the recently arrived boys joined the thirty-six girls in the chapel of the girls' dormitory.

"Where is James Whitaker? When is the last time anyone saw him?"

"William Murney was with him on the porch a little while ago, but William came inside. . . ."

"This is most disturbing," Mother Camillus said. "We absolutely must keep everyone together. Henry!" She called down the hallway. "Henry! A word, please."

Henry Esquior had just come in after spending the last half hour searching the grounds for his horse, who had panicked and run off. He poked his head in the chapel door. "Yes, ma'am?"

"Henry," Mother Camillus said, "I need you to go outside and get some clothesline."

Henry stared at her blankly, water dripping from his stubbly face.

"We need something to tie ourselves to the children, in

case . . . in case we take in too much water. We'll need to be able to lead them to safety."

Henry nodded. "I'll get the line."

"And Henry, please be on the lookout for James Whitaker. We're missing him."

Henry nodded and walked once again into the storm.

Mother Camillus assessed the situation in her chapel. The ten Sisters were scattered among the ninety children, doing their best to keep them calm.

Young Maggie looked panicked. Albert held her hand and spoke softly to her.

"See, we're all together now, everyone is OK." But Maggie was having none of it. She pointed to Tony, scuttling into the pew in front of them alongside Frank. He was still carrying the bloody pillow, and the cuts on his face looked raw.

Albert stared at Tony and wondered what had happened. He stroked Maggie's hand.

"OK, children," Mother Camillus yelled over the chatter that had erupted in the chapel in the wake of the boys' entrance. Clapping her hands together, she exclaimed, "Let's sing!"

The hesitant strains of "Queen of the Waves" began to overtake the sound of children asking questions and Sisters offering comfort. Mother Camillus sang loudly and gestured with her arms to encourage the children. She walked along the aisles, nodding to the Sisters she passed and indicating with her puffed-out chest that they should sing louder.

Henry returned, dripping wet, with clothesline in his hands. Seeing him, Mother Camillus tapped Sister Elizabeth on the shoulder, whispered in her ear, and handed her a pair of scissors. Sister Elizabeth rose and walked to the back of the chapel, where she and Henry began cutting the clothesline into long sections. A few minutes later Sister Elizabeth, still singing, walked down the aisles and started handing the other Sisters pieces of clothesline.

"Children," Mother Camillus bellowed over the singing from the front of the chapel, "I need you to listen to the Sisters and do what they tell you."

Frank turned to Tony, whose eyes were red from crying. Tony was trembling.

"Smile, Tony-boy!" Frank said, mussing Tony's hair. "Don't tucker yourself out cryin'. You know the day after a storm is sure enough sunny! We'll be playing ball by the dunes tomorrow, just you wait."

A booming sound erupted over the roar of the storm. Henry darted out of the chapel and followed the fearful roar down the hallway. He stopped dead in his tracks in front of the window over-looking the boys' dormitory, which had so recently been evacuated.

The tide had swallowed it.

CANDLES AND MISSILES

SAM SAT UPSTAIRS IN AN armchair, eyes closed, listening to the storm roar outside. The wind was full of noises he'd never heard before—the sounds of the planet rearranging, turning itself inside out.

This is chaos, Sam thought. The laws of the universe had been overturned. Trees flew through the air. Houses sank like ships. The Gulf of Mexico had invaded his living room. Soon it would climb the stairs.

On the east side of his house he heard a heavy thumping. He opened his eyes into darkness, his unlit candle in his hand.

Sam lit it and followed the sound of the thumping into the hallway.

Daisy returned to the parlor clutching her bag of coins. A few of the candles had gone out, so she took one lit candle and circulated around the room to relight them. Mrs. Hesse was curled up in a chair in the corner, crying quietly. The rest of the guests were eerily quiet, standing listening to the storm, holding hands, talking in hushed tones. Then there were the cats.

All five cats huddled together under the cabinet, crying. Over and over, they cried themselves out, went silent . . . until the wind hurled something against the building and the cries began anew. Danny knelt down next to the cabinet and held his hand out to pet them but only got hissed at in return. Button and Sherlock fled the cabinet and hopped on Aunt Talia's lap, snarling at each other over who would get the best seat. Talia winced as the claws dug into her skin.

Alice came back into the parlor, her horrified face lit by the candle in her hand. Daisy walked over to her.

"Mother," she whispered, "you look like you've seen a ghost."

"Well, I certainly would have preferred that, dear," she said softly. "Come with me."

Alice and Daisy walked out of the parlor to the staircase. Peering down, Daisy saw that the water had risen nearly two-thirds of the way up. Magazines and doilies floated on the surface.

Daisy gasped. "Dear God, what are we to do?"

She realized that she had been wrong to shield their guests from the truth. She had been afraid to set off a panic at the time, but now she would have to tell them not only that water was in the building but also that it was more than halfway up the stairs.

There might be no escaping this storm, Daisy thought. She clasped the coin purse in her hand tightly, as if it were a good-luck charm.

"We're just going to have to tell everyone," Alice whispered. "It's as simple as that."

They stood watching the water rise in the stairwell, spooked into silence. Then Alice took Daisy's hand and led her back into the parlor. As they prepared to walk into the room, they both heard a scraping sound behind them.

Daisy whipped her head around and saw a dark shape on the floor at the top of the stairs. She crept closer and bent down as the scraping continued.

"Daisy, what is it?"

Approaching the shape, Daisy held out her candle. Alice leaned in, then slapped her hand over her mouth.

A dead raccoon was bobbing at the top of the stairs, its claws scratching against the floor as it moved on the water.

Daisy dropped the candle and it went out. As it rolled along the floor, she grabbed her mother by the arm in the darkness and walked her back to the parlor.

———◆———

Eighteen blocks west, Charlie clung to the tree as the wind ripped the shirt off of his back. He was so close to home, just a few blocks away. But he didn't dare let go of the tree to try and get there. Even if he managed it . . . was his house still standing?

Charlie lifted his head against the wind, trying to gain a view of the houses along the street. Many had already collapsed. It was hard to distinguish even one pile of timber from the next. There was no difference between street and yard. Houses, wagons, tool-sheds, bicycles—everything was being gnarled by the storm into a jumble of debris. In the distance Charlie could see people fleeing in boats, unable to control the direction they sailed in.

Then the tree itself began to move, wrenched from the ground by the relentless wind. The tree began to shake more and more furiously. He closed his eyes and prayed. He imagined that his mother, grandmother, and little brother had somehow made

A portrait of Sister Vincent with two orphans, circa 1890s

it to safety; that his father had stopped working early enough to seek shelter. He also prayed that Sam Young was OK.

Charlie's prayers were interrupted when the tree broke loose from the ground. He clung to the tree as it was seized by the wind and screamed as it was hurled into the air, now another rogue missile in the storm's arsenal.

⸻ ◆ ⸻

Screams erupted inside the chapel after the explosive crash outside the girls' dormitory. Frank looked out the window and saw pieces of the boys' dormitory floating past. "It's our building!" he yelled, setting off a chain reaction of screams and shouts. Mother Camillus struggled to be heard as she implored the children to be calm.

Henry returned to the chapel, walking through water up to his shins. He stood outside the closed chapel door, not wanting to scare the children by letting in the water that had pushed its way into the building. As Henry reached out to open the door, Sister Elizabeth opened it from the inside, and water flowed into the chapel, splashing across the floor.

Standing in the aisle, waiting for instructions from Mother Camillus, Maggie screamed and squeezed Albert's hand as water rushed over her feet.

"Children! Please follow the Sisters' directions! We must tie ourselves together! I want all the older children to help the Sisters with the younger ones! Quickly!"

The children were terrified. Some of them began to cry as the Sisters tied the younger ones together with the clothesline and then threaded the remaining rope through their own garments and tied it around their waists. Albert stood behind Maggie in the aisle with his hands on her shoulders. He kissed the top of her head while she stared in horror as Sister Raphael secured the line around the arms of some of the children.

All the while the Sisters tried to keep the children singing "Queen of the Waves." Sister Vincent finished tying herself to eight children, little Joseph Murney among them. She instructed the group to join hands, and they began swaying back and forth.

"And left, and right, and left, and right, and sing!" Sister Vincent exclaimed, trying in vain to distract the children from the sounds of the storm.

William stood next to Joseph, though he wasn't tied to the group. He tried to assist Sister Vincent in getting the group to sway and sing.

"Joe!" he yelled at his brother. Joseph looked tearfully at William, who started doing an exaggerated, though silent, impression of an opera singer belting out an aria, his arms reaching to the heavens and his eyes shut tight. Joseph blinked and pushed out a few more tears, but when he opened his eyes again, he was laughing.

Sister Elizabeth successfully tied seven children together and approached Maggie with the line. Maggie backed away.

"Maggie, darling, please. I'm doing this to keep you safe," Sister Elizabeth coaxed.

Albert tried to help. "Come on, sis, I'll be right here with you." Maggie shook her head.

"Here, I'll let Sister tie me up too. How about that?"

She shook her head more fiercely this time and backed away from her brother.

"Maggie, please!" Albert said, stepping forward and reaching out his arm.

She turned and ran out of the chapel.

* * *

THUMP.

Ghostly shadows conjured by the candle Sam carried danced on the wall at the top of the stairs. They danced wildly in response to rogue gusts of wind coming through cracks in the walls.

THUMP.

The noise was coming from below. Sam looked at the shadows on the wall, then down at the flickering candle flame, twisted by the wind shooting through the air. As he approached the stairs, he saw that the light from the candle was itself dancing on something . . . on water. Yes, water had reached the top of the stairs.

THUMP. THUMP.

Sam knelt down, shining the light from the candle over the surface of the water, casting an otherworldly glow across the hallway. Something dark was floating a few feet below the waterline. The piano bench.

THUMP. THUMP.

The bench knocked against the railing of the staircase, and suddenly Sam realized what was happening below. The furniture in one of the lower bedrooms was slamming against the ceiling.

Sam marveled again at how quickly the rules of the universe had changed. Up was down. Inside was out. Outside was in. Right now, every object he called to mind—a teakettle, an outhouse, a door, a person—was doing something it was not meant to do: fly through the air. Not even his sturdily constructed house would be left alone. The house was becoming a ship. And the ship would go down.

The house groaned and shook. Sam turned to the balcony door behind him. The only means of escape. The water was on its way up—he needed to get out before it was too late.

———◦•◦———

"Irene! Irene!" Mrs. Hesse screamed at the parlor window as she saw pieces of her house sail past on the water.

Daisy leaned against the doorway, her eyes roaming from person to person in the parlor. She thought back to last night: she had planned on going for an evening swim, had even put her suit on and walked down to the beach. But she'd decided against getting in the water after watching the aggressive waves beat against the shore. Now she wished she had gone in the water anyway. It might have been her last chance to swim. Voluntarily, that is.

She knelt down and took Aunt Talia's hand. Talia was breathing heavily, obviously scared, and stroking Button and Sherlock. Daisy felt a pang of guilt, thinking back to her frustration at having to liberate her aunt's cats from the living room. Aunt Talia was never very good at keeping her wits about her in stressful situations.

Except for Mrs. Hesse and the cats scattered around the room, none of the more than twenty people crowded into the parlor made a noise above a whisper. Even Danny, still crouched down next to the cabinet, was sitting quietly and not peppering Daisy and Alice with questions as he usually did. It was as if everyone was hoping that, if they were quiet enough, if they just held on and kept their voices down for long enough, the murderous storm outside would leave them alone and go on to the next house. They occasionally glanced resentfully at Mrs. Hesse, as if she were drawing the storm's attention.

For the first time in her life Daisy felt completely adrift, with absolutely no idea what the best course of action might be. She'd been sure the storm would blow over. The water was rising outside to a level that was unimaginable this morning. Should they try to seek shelter in the apartment on the third floor? Should they huddle in Daisy's room? Or should they just stay put and hope they made the right decision when the storm finally did its worst? Because Daisy had a terrible feeling that the worst was yet to come. And soon.

Daisy stood up just as the apartment started shaking and the sounds of falling bricks and concrete filled the room. Afraid the floor might collapse, Daisy backed herself against the wall. But though she could feel the building shaking, the floor remained intact. A few of the parlor guests shrieked, fearing the worst.

But the shrieks were eclipsed by white-hot screams erupting in the apartment next door.

Daisy looked at her mother. "We never checked on the McCauleys...."

———◆———

"Maggie!" Albert shouted after his sister as she darted out of the chapel. He dashed after her, sloshing through several feet of water. It was dark in the hallway, and he couldn't see where she'd gone.

"Maggie!" Thinking she had gone to hide in the dorm room she shared with nine other girls, he felt along the wall for doorknobs as he walked, counting them until he came to her room. He opened the door.

"Maggie! Maggie, come on, now!" He could see no movement inside, only the shuddering of the walls from the relentless pressure of the wind. The windowpanes seemed as if they were about to shatter. He walked in, water up to his knees, and felt his way to the row of beds against the wall, touching the tops of all of them, searching for his sister. She wasn't there.

He shut the door and walked toward the center of the long building. Albert saw her standing in the center of the large entrance room, her outline visible against the windows, illuminated by flashes of lightning outside. She stood looking out at the sky, transfixed by the raging storm and the projectiles of varying shapes and sizes flying past.

"Come on, sis. The Sisters are just making sure they can keep all of us safe, in case . . ." He looked out the window. "In case something happens."

Maggie looked at Albert with wet eyes, and he could see her lips trembling.

"Aw, Maggie, you know I'll be right beside you. Here, take my hand."

Maggie looked back outside. Reluctantly, she took her brother's hand, and together they walked back to the chapel.

Inside, the singing had been replaced by crying and shouting, while the Sisters asked the children to be calm. Groups of children were now tied to each other. Sister Elizabeth saw Albert leading Maggie back and smiled. "Maggie, come here, love!"

Albert and Maggie walked to the south wall where Sister Elizabeth had gathered her group. There were seven tied to her, and Maggie would make eight.

Unable to help herself, Maggie started to cry. Albert placed his hands on her shoulders and gently nudged her toward Sister Elizabeth.

"Maggie, I'll be right here," he assured her.

"Sweet Maggie," Elizabeth said, "I will keep you right next to me, OK, love? You'll be right by my side. I'm not going to let go of you, OK?"

Through tears and twitching lips, Maggie said, "OK."

"That's my girl. Come along, now, let's get you in position."

Sister Elizabeth placed Maggie at the end of the line of children, separating her from Albert.

"Give me your hand, love."

Maggie looked at Sister Elizabeth and over at her brother. Albert nodded. Maggie held out her hand and Sister Elizabeth tied the clothesline around her wrist.

————◆————

The wind scraped and moaned against Sam Young's second-floor balcony door. He knew that the time had come to fight. He had no armor and no weapons to fend off the leviathan outside. This was clear. All he had was a plan . . . but he knew that plans could be thwarted.

Sam looked behind him. The water was coming for him, up the stairs, and quickly. There was no other choice. He said a quiet prayer and pulled the door open.

The water surged in, hurling him against the wall.

BALANCING ACT

At Lucas Terrace the crowd in the Thornes' candlelit parlor trembled at the wails of people sailing past the building on the tide. Alice went to the cabinet and pulled out the family Bible.

She looked at Daisy as she opened it, and Daisy nodded. Alice flipped through the Bible to the Book of Psalms.

The thumping of the living room furniture against the ceiling got louder, the shaking of the building more convulsive. Alice began to read aloud:

"The Lord is my shepherd, I shall not want. . . ."

———✦———

The darkened chapel at the orphanage shook, and the water continued to rise. The Sisters had finally managed to get all of the younger children tied together in groups. The water was high and rising—the time had come to move to the second floor.

Mother Camillus addressed her flock from the front of the chapel, this time flanked by the children tied to her waist. Henry stood beside her with a toddler on his back.

"Children, quickly, we must go upstairs! Quickly, now. Everyone hold hands with the person next to you!"

Maggie looked fearfully at Albert, who now stood in front of her, though he wasn't tied to the others in her group. "I'll stay with you, sis," he said.

William and Joseph stood together with Sister Vincent's group. William had given up trying to distract Joseph from the storm and was now trying to keep his brother from accidentally untying himself from the group as he fidgeted with the clothesline around his wrist.

Frank left Tony with Sister Elizabeth's group. He snuck out of the chapel and up the stairs, determined to get to the roof and see what the storm had done. Behind him, even over the raucous sounds of the storm, he heard Mother Camillus's voice echoing through the darkness.

The Sisters and the children filed out of the chapel, each nun holding a candle. As they made their way toward the staircase, Mother Camillus addressed the children.

"Now let's give thanks to the Lord for keeping us safe! 'Queen of the Waves'! Lift up your voices, everyone!"

Mother Camillus began singing the first verse. The Sisters quickly joined her. Slowly the children began to sing along, and by the second verse, the singing echoed throughout the dormitory as ten nuns and more than ninety children climbed the stairs by candlelight.

Up to thy shrine we look and see the glimmer
Thy votive lamp sheds down on us afar;
Light of our eyes, oh let it ne'er grow dimmer
Till in the sky we hail the morning star.

With the singing resounding below him, Frank climbed up a ladder leading to the roof's trap door. He pushed hard, struggling against the wind. Finally he was able to shove the door open and poke his head out. As he pulled himself onto the roof, a piece of timber flying through the air came down on him, sending him rolling to the edge.

* * *

In the apartment next to Daisy's, Jane McCauley screamed for the Lord to show mercy as the bedroom shook. She held tightly to her husband, Jim, who was lying on the bed on the second floor of their apartment. A wall downstairs had collapsed, causing the floor beneath them to rattle and creak. Jane reached for Jim's wheelchair as it rolled away and out of her grasp. Jane and Jim looked at each other fearfully, knowing that it was only a matter of time before the floor gave way, sending them tumbling amid an avalanche of bricks and concrete.

Two other people crouched in the corner trembling. Louisa and Katherine Drake, twenty-one-year-old twin sisters, lived in the apartment next to the McCauleys, and they had sought refuge in the McCauley apartment after theirs had taken in too much water.

"We've got to get out of here!" Louisa shouted.

"But where can we go?" her sister replied.

Jane stood up. "We'll have to cross to the other wing."

Lucas Terrace was an L-shaped building, with one wing running along Broadway facing south and the other running along Sixth Street facing east. Both the McCauley and Thorne apartments sat at the corner where the two wings met, the Thorne apartment facing south and the McCauley place facing east. Both apartments took up the first two floors of the building, each with another apartment on the third floor. In order to get to the other wing, the McCauleys and the Drake girls would have to somehow get into the apartment above them and cross over its balcony to the balcony above the Thorne apartment. For someone in Jim McCauley's condition, this seemed like an impossible task.

"Let's go," Jane said resolutely. A strong woman who had taken care of her paralyzed husband for almost twenty years, she made decisions quickly and didn't often change her mind.

"Darling," Jim said softly. "Please, I'll stay here. You all go on. . . ."

"Nonsense!"

Katherine protested. "But Jane, . . . cross to the other wing? How?"

Jane grabbed Katherine and Louisa by the arms and directed them to a door leading out to the building's side stairwell. "And what about Mr. McCauley?" Katherine and Louisa looked at Jim as he lay on the bed, his wheelchair against the opposite wall.

"We've got to go up—all of us!" Jane said. "To the balcony! Up and over!"

Katherine and Louisa looked at Jane like she was crazy.

———— ◆ ————

Sam Young lifted his head as the water flooded his hallway. He moved toward the open balcony door, grabbing the doorknob. Clinging with both hands, he drew himself through the incoming tide and out onto the balcony, catching hold of a shutter on the side of the house.

The roar of the wind was awful. Against sheets of blinding rain, Sam stood on the teetering balcony. With one hand

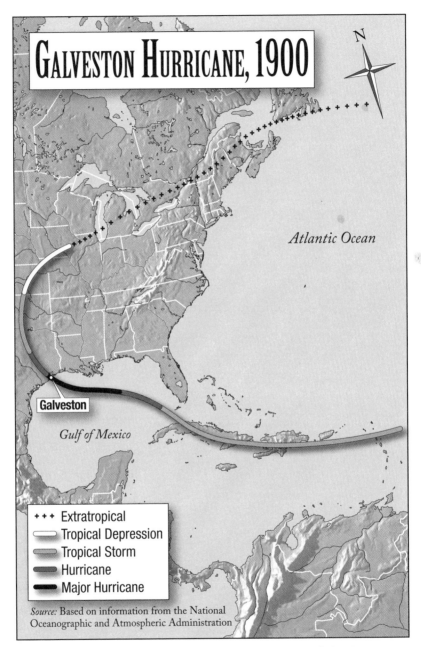

GALVESTON HURRICANE, 1900

N

Atlantic Ocean

Galveston

Gulf of Mexico

+ + + Extratropical
Tropical Depression
Tropical Storm
Hurricane
Major Hurricane

Source: Based on information from the National
Oceanographic and Atmospheric Administration

The path of the hurricane, which reached full strength over Galveston

holding tightly to the shutter and the other shielding his eyes, he looked right and left. Only his house and the Youenses' house next door still stood. Their homes looked like two misshapen schooners lost in the middle of the Gulf of Mexico.

It was the grandest and most horrific site Sam had ever seen. "Mr. Youens," Sam said with a sigh, relieved that his neighbor and his family might still be alive. He had seen them boarding up their windows in the afternoon.

But even as Sam watched, the Youenses' house came unmoored. It drifted forward, turned partly around and then tilted upward, as if it were being lifted at one corner by an invisible rope. The house hung suspended for a few seconds, until the wind shifted direction violently, whirling the house around. Clinging to the shutter of his own house, Sam's heart pounded as the Youenses' house was swept away, disappearing from sight.

Water poured through Sam's balcony door from the inside out, gushing like a hundred fire hoses.

Just one block away a tree slammed through the roof of a house on Q Street.

The tree had a passenger: Charlie. The top of the tree snapped off, sending the bottom trunk down into the water, leaning against the side of the damaged house. Charlie looked down from the limb of the tree and couldn't believe his luck. He looked around for signs of life inside, but the house seemed to be abandoned. Fearing that the wind might change direction again and send him flying, he climbed down and jumped into the water. He grabbed the porch railing and pulled himself along. He could feel the structure give a little. This house, he could tell, would be gone soon. He swam frantically toward the next house, which he knew was the Clevelands', whom he had also done some work for. It was then that he realized how close he was to Sam Young's house, just a few blocks away. He had spent the past few hours trying to get home but now was no closer to it than when he'd begun.

Approaching the porch, he could see three darkened figures pushing their way through the front door, moving through water up to their armpits. Charlie made his way toward the Cleveland house, his head still barely above the water, when suddenly there was a crash behind him. A small boat had blown into the tree he'd just climbed down from. This proved fatal for the house next door, which folded in on itself and collapsed into the water.

Charlie waded up the steps, onto the porch, and into the Clevelands' rattling home.

"Go upstairs and see if you can find a way in," Jane told Louisa and Katherine. The McCauleys' apartment at Lucas Terrace was quickly disintegrating. "Use the side stairwell. I've got to get Jim."

Jane grabbed the wheelchair that had rolled into the far wall and dragged it over to the bed. As Jim protested, she hoisted him into the chair, then wheeled him out to the stairwell. Louisa and Katherine had already reached the third floor. The door of the apartment was off its hinges, allowing the girls to push it through the threshold and into the living room. Jane hauled Jim up the stairs in his wheelchair, climbing the steps backward while dragging the chair with her, her strong arms keeping him tilted upward as they ascended.

Louisa and Katherine ventured through the abandoned

apartment and stopped at the balcony doors. Through the darkness they could see the apartment's balcony and the one just a few feet beyond it, which belonged to the apartment next door. That's the chasm they needed to bridge.

"Girls!" Jane shouted. She needed help maneuvering Jim's wheelchair through the trash-strewn apartment.

Katharine and Louisa struggled to help move Jim through to the balcony doors, when Jane caught sight of an ironing board leaning against the wall.

"Look!" she said, pointing at the board. "We can use that!" Jane pointed to it, indicating that Katharine should go fetch it. Jim had given up protesting, all too aware of how stubborn his wife could be.

Jane walked around the chair to face her husband. She bent at the knees, grasped Jim by the arms, and pulled him to his feet, holding him steady. She turned around, took his arms and positioned them on her shoulders, bent at the knees again, and then hoisted him onto her back. She waited for one of the girls to open the balcony doors and place the ironing board in position.

"Let's go, ladies!"

Louisa grabbed the ironing board and Katherine opened the balcony door. The two stepped out into howling wind and driving rain, holding tightly to the ironing board. They placed it flat on the balcony railing and pushed it out, creating a bridge to the other balcony.

Jane carried Jim out onto the balcony and, with the girls' help, placed him on the end of the board as the wind tore at their clothes.

The girls helped Jane step over Jim and onto the board, all of them fighting to stay upright.

"Darling!" Jim shouted. "Save yourself! It's useless!"

"Nonsense!" Jane shouted back. "Your legs don't work, but you've got the strongest arms in town, my dear!"

Crouched down on the board, she carefully backed away from him toward the neighboring balcony. Following her lead, Jim pressed his hands against the board and lifted his lower body up. With his legs dangling over the rushing water, he pulled himself across the ironing board.

Katherine clapped her hands and yelped with excitement when Jane pulled him to safety, then stepped onto the board and scuttled across as her sister held it down against the balcony railing.

Jane hoisted Jim onto her back again and took him inside the apartment, while Katherine remained behind to help Louisa across.

Louisa clambered up onto the ironing board. From the other side Katherine leaned her weight against the board to keep it steady against the railing. Louisa slowly crawled across. Once she was more than halfway, Katherine reached out one hand toward her sister. Louisa grabbed it to pull herself to the other side. Louisa hopped off the board and onto the balcony, excited to have cleared that seemingly impossible hurdle. The girls turned to go inside when suddenly the wind changed direction and upturned the ironing board, smacking Louisa across the back and sending her flying over the balcony railing.

Louisa screamed as she plunged into the flood below.

<hr>

One of the balcony posts blew out and struck Sam in the head. He passed out for a few seconds, and when he awoke, his head was bleeding and pain shot through his skull. He looked around the balcony, searching for an option. The surge was coming. He knew it was coming. With one hand he tried to shield himself from the flapping of the balcony door against the side of the house. That's when the plan came to him.

The balcony door had been shaken and whipped so much by the wind that it was loose on its hinges. When the time came, he would rip the door off its hinges and use it as a raft. His head bleeding from the blow of the post, he grabbed the door with one hand so that he could be ready, keeping a grip on the shutter with the other.

He held on tight as the wind tore through the balcony, blowing the other posts away like straws and sending the railing flying. Before long, the rest of the balcony blew away, and Sam was flat against the side of the house, holding tightly to the shutter and the door.

It sounded like he was lying under a railroad bridge as a locomotive roared over him. If it got any louder, he was sure his head would split in two. He held on. He held his breath. He felt it coming.

He lifted his legs, slapped his feet against the side of the house, grabbed the door, and got ready to pull.

There was a banging on the side door upstairs in the Thorne apartment. Daisy rushed into the hall to open the door. There stood Jane, with Jim leaning against her and Katherine helping to hold him up. They looked like they'd been spat out by a whale.

Jane dragged Jim into Mrs. Thorne's bedroom, and a sobbing Katherine followed Daisy into the crowded parlor. The storm was hurling giant objects against the building now with increasing frequency, and the parlor floor quaked. Everyone in the room heard the sound of the apartments next door falling.

"We've got to get out of this room!" Mrs. Hesse shouted.

"But where do we go?" Gus asked.

"There's no place that's safe!" Emma shouted.

"The third floor is probably better," Robert said, looking up. "What say we try to make our way up there?"

"No!" Lilly Morton yelled. She and her brother, Kyle, had been huddling in the corner with their parents, and she had been crying.

"Daisy," Robert continued, ignoring Lilly, "do you know your upstairs neighbors? Are they at home?"

"I think the MacMillans are out of town," Daisy answered. She looked around at the people in the room, struggling to make out a consensus opinion. "We could all go into my room," Daisy said. "It's at the end of the hall."

"Daisy's right, I think that is our best option," Alice chimed in.

Chatter about what to do erupted through the room, even as the storm banged on the walls of the parlor.

"Everyone please, please listen!" Daisy shouted over the din. "I think my room is the safest place," Daisy said. "It's on the side away from the Gulf." As she talked, Daisy bent down to try to lift Button out of her aunt's lap, but the cat hissed and scuttled under the chair.

The room was paralyzed with indecision.

Daisy looked down at the cracking floor. "Well, that's that! To my room! Now! Everyone!"

All twenty-two people in the parlor hurried out into the hall and down to Daisy's bedroom as the parlor floor started giving way. Daisy helped her aunt Talia stand and hurry down the hall, pressing the people in front of her to move faster.

"Danny, hurry!" Daisy yelled back at her brother.

Danny stood alone in the threshold of the parlor looking at

the cats, all of whom had gathered in the far corner. There was no way he would be able to reach them. The center of the floor was now starting to crumble. He stepped backward as the floor in front of him gave way.

CITY OF THE DEAD

A COLOSSAL, 125-MILE-AN-HOUR WIND WAS making Galveston its plaything. It hurled the waters of the Gulf of Mexico across the city, lifting up giant ocean steamers weighing thousands of tons like toys, smashing them through bridges and dashing them against bluffs on the Texas mainland, like a five-hundred-foot monster throwing a temper tantrum.

Frank clung to the roof of the girls' dormitory, but the wind pulled his body away from the building, almost parallel to the ground. Just as he began to lose his grip, the wind reversed course, whipping him back onto the roof. Frank scurried back to the trapdoor, stricken by what he had seen: the building looked like it was floating in the middle of the Gulf. There was no land in sight.

Frank opened the trapdoor and slid down the ladder. He heard the nuns and children singing in the darkness and marveled that such a beautiful sound could exist amid such chaos. A few older boys were at the base of the ladder wanting to climb up, and they peppered him with questions.

"Hey! What happened? What did you see?"

"You don't want to go out there!" Frank said, but the boys pushed him aside and climbed the ladder. They opened the trap door and clambered out, leaving the door flapping open.

"Hey!" Frank jumped back on the ladder. "Hey, get back down here!"

Down the hall Albert stood with Maggie and her group. There were only a few candles still burning.

"Sis, just think about Topeka, huh?" Albert said. "We'll be there in just a few weeks! Mary Anne and Uncle George are fixing their house up real nice for us! And they ain't got no storms like this there, neither."

For the first time that day, Maggie smiled. She grabbed her brother's hand and swung it forward playfully.

"Children, let us pray!" Mother Camillus shouted. "Bow your heads, children! Bow your heads!"

Children cried as the storm shook the building more and more violently. Some of them bowed their heads; others couldn't keep themselves from looking around, squinting their eyes to see through the darkness.

Standing next to a window, Joseph bowed his head, but he couldn't keep his eyes closed. Suddenly, he felt the floor shift beneath him, as if it was being shaken loose from the rest of the building. A few children fell to the floor, bringing the orphans they were tied to down with them. Tugged toward the floor by the child next to him, Joseph struggled to stay on his feet. He looked up—the ceiling was sagging downward while the far wall was leaning farther and farther away. Outside, a monstrous surge of water approached the building. Joseph squeezed William's hand.

The boys on the roof screamed.

The Thorne apartment at Lucas Terrace still stood, but it was crumbling more with every passing second. Danny jumped backward into the hallway as the parlor floor started to break apart and the trapped cats shrieked. He dashed down the hallway to Daisy's room, narrowly avoiding slamming into Daisy on her way out.

"Danny, help with Auntie. She's in a panic. I've put her on the bed." Danny squeezed into the tiny, overcrowded bedroom and pushed through to the side of the bed, where Aunt Talia was lying down and Alice stood over her, fanning her with her

A hurricane-flooded house typical of the early 20th century

hands. Something had already crashed through the window, and everyone crouched and tried to shield themselves from flying bricks, timber, and other wreckage that threatened to sail through.

Daisy went to her mother's room to get some pillows to help shield Alice and Talia from the debris. She trod lightly on the deteriorating hallway floor, aware that it could collapse at any moment.

Jim McCauley lay on Daisy's mother's bed, while his wife, Jane, sat next to him and stroked his head. "Mr. and Mrs. McCauley, you really must come to the other room!" Daisy shouted over the roar of the wind. "The floor is giving way, there's not much time!"

Jane looked down at Jim, who was lying with his head on the pillow. She smiled.

"Darling?" She touched Jim's cheek.

"I can help you carry him, Mrs. McCauley, but we have to go now! Now!"

"Let's stay," Jim whispered. "Here. Together."

"OK." Jane grabbed his hand and clasped it to her chest.

"Mrs. McCauley!" Daisy cried. "Mrs. McCauley!"

But Jane didn't look up. She sat on the bed, gazing at her husband. Cats howled in the distance. The crackling beginnings of a thunderous eruption sounded in the hall.

Daisy turned and ran to her room, her footsteps barely staying ahead of the disintegrating hallway floor. As she slid into her room, the hallway behind her collapsed.

Charlie made his way into the darkened house full of refugees. The living room was packed with people, too many to count—wet, shivering shadows, all standing in four feet of water. A handful of people held candles, allowing Charlie to see a few terrified faces as he waded in and tried to find a place to stand.

The house creaked and trembled as it was pummeled by gusts of wind and rain and flying objects from collapsing houses. Charlie leaned against a wall for the briefest of moments before it started crumbling. He stood up quickly and moved through the room to an empty hallway, but he soon understood why no one was there: the backside of the house, including the kitchen and dining room, had been ripped off. At the end of the hall, Charlie had a clear view of the backyard—a wild cavalcade of flying furniture and disintegrating houses. The wind shrieked as it flung debris here, there, and everywhere.

This house will fall soon, he thought.

Charlie dodged a chair that came at his face, lost his footing, and slipped under the water. Leaping up, he grabbed onto a beam hanging in the remains of the collapsed wall that had divided the living room and kitchen.

He pulled himself up, up, up, onto the second floor, which now looked out over the water, since the back of the house had been ripped away. He rushed to find a way to the roof, figuring that was the safest place to be. All he could think was that he had to escape the water, and the only way to go was up.

Finding a set of stairs to the roof, he leaped up them two at a time, alighting on the roof just as the house began its last pirouette and surrendered to the sea. He felt the ground shift beneath him and frantically looked around for something in the water to use as a raft.

A violent gust of wind smacked Charlie off the crumbling house. He flew into the air and was hurled against the roof of a capsizing house across the street.

Charlie's lifeless body slid down into the water headfirst.

Sam was poised to push off the side of his house: he pressed his body to the doorway and planted his feet firmly on either side of the balcony door. One hand gripped one side of the door, and the other hand was ready to pull the other side off its hinges.

Time seemed to have slowed down, and Sam struggled to hold himself in position. He couldn't believe that his house, as beat up as it was, was still standing. But it surely wouldn't be for long. Would it?

He lifted his head and gazed through the threshold into the upstairs hallway facing him. Inside he saw what looked like electrical sparks bouncing off the wall. Was that possible? No, couldn't be. The interior of the house was underwater!

Phosphorescence, he thought. Yes, it was water—drops of seawater giving off absorbed energy in the form of light. Or maybe the high wind was giving off electricity. Whatever the cause, it was a gorgeous sight. The drops of rain were becoming luminous as they struck the wall. It looked like a miniature fireworks display.

Sam closed his eyes and put his head down. He was finding it increasingly difficult to breathe. The wind, he thought, must be blowing 125 miles an hour now. He opened his eyes again, but he could no longer see the luminescent water. He could no longer see much of anything.

The wind blew harder and harder, as if it were impatient at

the house's refusal to fall. Barely able to feel his hands gripping the door, he began to feel that he was already flying through the air. No, not flying. Being thrown.

Sam cried out to God. He didn't know how much longer he could hold on. All of a sudden, he felt a jerk underneath him as the house finally yielded. This was it. With a firm hold of the door and both feet planted against the house, he used all his strength to pull the door completely from its hinges. A wave surge finally overtook the house and spat it into the air.

Frank watched in horror from the bottom of the ladder: the boys who had managed to make it to the roof of the girls' dorm were ripped away by a twenty-foot wave. Their screams were heard by the children and nuns inside. Everyone soon felt the dizzying sensation of the building being lifted up. It began to float uneasily on the tide as screams pierced the darkness and the dormitory swayed and pulsated.

Through the darkness, the commanding voice of Mother Camillus rose above the cacophony of cries and shrieks:

Help, then sweet Queen, in our exceeding danger,
By thy seven griefs, in pity Lady save;
Think of the Babe that slept within the manger
And help us now, dear Lady of the Wave.

Time seemed to freeze in the dark. There was no more candle-light. Everyone tried not to move.

Albert held tightly to Maggie's hand. "Maggie, I'm right here! Don't let go of me!" The sounds of children's cries rang out through the hallway. Albert heard one child near him sobbing to Sister Elizabeth.

"Sister, please don't let go! Please don't let go!"

"I'll hold you tightly, darling! Very tightly! Close your eyes and pray now! Pray!"

The storm that had finally made its way up to the second floor of the dormitory screeched and whipped itself through the hall as Mother Camillus's voice rang out.

Up to thy shrine we look and see the glimmer
Thy votive lamp sheds down on us afar;
Light of our eyes, oh let it ne'er grow dimmer,
Till in the sky we hail the morning star.

William let go of Joseph's hand so he could throw his arms around his brother and make sure the others connected to the clothesline didn't lead him away. In the instant he let Joseph's hand go, he was jerked away by the other children as they moved down the hall.

"Joseph! Joseph!" William called frantically in the dark, but he couldn't hear an answer.

Nearby, Albert held strong to Maggie's hand. One of the children she was tied to lost his balance and fell over, bringing some of the children down with him and knocking Sister Elizabeth off balance. Maggie remained on her feet, clinging to her brother's hand even as her other wrist was pulled toward the floor.

As the wall rattled and the floor began to crumble, Mother Camillus sang out.

Then joyful hearts shall kneel around thine altar

And grateful psalms re-echo down the nave;
Never our faith in thy sweet power can falter,
Mother of God, our La—

After less than a minute of floating in the Gulf, the bottom dropped out of the dormitory, the floor gave way, and the walls collapsed.

In the crumbling Thorne apartment, Jane sat with Jim on Alice Thorne's bed. The hallway connecting them to the others in Daisy's room had now collapsed, and they were left alone.

Looking out into what used to be the hallway, Jane saw the waters of the Gulf flowing into the building.

She looked down at Jim, who was trembling.

"Rest easy, darling," she said.

Standing on the other end of the apartment at the edge of her bedroom was Daisy. She clung to the threshold of the room as she heard cries and screams behind her. Holding the door open, she could see Jane and Jim in her mother's bedroom, separated from her by a river of rushing water where the hallway used to be, with no bridge connecting her to them. She let out a little yelp as the reality of their plight set in. She looked down at her hand, which to her surprise still held the little velvet change purse. It was wet from sweat and sprays of salt water.

"Daisy! Daisy, get away from the doorway!" Alice called from beside Daisy's bed, where Aunt Talia lay shell-shocked. She could see large pieces of wood and metal flying through the air very close to where Daisy stood. In an instant a giant section of the ceiling was ripped off.

Timber from a neighboring lumberyard flew into the side of Lucas Terrace like a spray of tomahawks and the entire east wing collapsed. A great ripping sound erupted on the other side of the apartment, the only other part of the building still standing. Daisy looked out to where she had just seen Jane and Jim.

Her mother's room had fallen, and the McCauleys were gone. Daisy slammed her bedroom door against the invading tide.

A great wave, twenty feet high, surged into the island city of Galveston at approximately 7:30 p.m. If the heavens had had the power of sight at that moment, they would have witnessed as many varieties of violent and random death as could be imagined. But even as it was destroyed, Galveston put up a fight. Its sturdy beachfront structures collapsed into each other as they were pushed inland, combining forces to create an enormous bulwark against the gushing Gulf.

The great waves swept one house against the other against the other against the other. The entire beachfront district was pushed back, house against house, farther into Galveston. Several hundred yards of houses piled into each other like battering rams, compressed, gnarled, and pulverized into a great wall one hundred feet thick and thirty feet high. Meeting this barrier, the incoming waters from the Gulf spun around in whirlpools. Hundreds of victims were caught between the houses and crushed and drowned as the buildings slammed together.

At the time of the great surge, those who had fled their houses and ventured north or west to the business district, six to eight blocks from the beach, successfully outran the inrushing water, which was not deep enough there to drown a person who still had legs to run on. But there was no outrunning the wind and the missiles it launched: sheets of metal, slabs of concrete, bricks, mortar, timber, beds, pianos, animals. All were seized by the churning wind and hurled into the air. Heads were sliced off bodies by roofing shingles. People fleeing their crumbling houses were impaled by flying street signs or timber from collapsed houses. The wind ripped a five-month-old baby from its mother's arms as she ran down the street, carrying the infant away into the darkness.

Meanwhile, those like Sam Young who remained in their houses on the beach side, within four blocks of the Gulf, faced the full violence of both wind and water. Their faith in the sturdiness of their homes often proved fatal. At the moment the great wave overtook the island and the houses began to rise, tilt, and bob on the engorged tide, these true believers emerged to swim for their lives. Strong people like Sam could seize giant, sturdy timbers or large slabs of housing and try to float to safety, but the physically weaker ones—women, children, the elderly—used what they could find for rafts: small pieces of house framing, flimsy sections of flooring or ceiling, chunks of roofs, furniture.

The storm took possession of every stretch of land on Galveston Island, hurling its citizens into the turbulent water. This included the sacred ground where Galveston's dead were laid to rest. Apparently not satisfied with the destruction of Galveston's living, the storm demanded that past generations also know its power. In cemeteries across the city, the dead were torn from their graves and from aboveground vaults. These vaults—a sort of a city of the dead within Galveston—were built of stone, concrete, and iron, but they were uprooted and scattered about the burial grounds with the same violence that attended the houses of the living. Metal caskets were seized from their tombs and their contents given up to the insatiable storm. Bodies of the long dead were adrift on the tide, knocking against those lost souls still clinging to life or those who had recently surrendered.

Both past and present were caught in the same horrific whirlpool. Now Galveston truly was a city of the dead. But the living still held on, ignorant of how lucky they were to still be alive and dreadfully aware of how unlucky they yet could be.

TREES IN THE WATER

SAM'S HOUSE ROSE SEVERAL FEET out of the water, a mortally wounded sea creature sucking in its last breath, before being seized by the wind and whisked away. On top of the door he had ripped from the house—the only remaining piece of his home—Sam looked at the water, the wind beating down so hard that the surface was almost completely flat, like glass. He lowered his head onto the door and exhaled.

Miles to the west William floated in the Gulf, his head bleeding from being struck by debris when the dormitory collapsed. He had been holding Joseph's hand only a second ago. Where was his brother now? Lost in the darkness. Tied to seven other children and Sister Vincent.

There was no more screaming, no more praying. Just the sound of the wind lashing the water. Blood covered William's face as he struggled to keep his head above the water. He grabbed hold of a sofa cushion rushing by and pulled his upper

Lucas Terrace after the storm

body onto it, struggling to keep steady as the cushion moved along with the current.

———

Frank Madera gasped as his head breached the surface of the water. He caught hold of a large piece of timber floating past, grabbing it with both arms and wrapping his body around it. He held on as it turned over and over in the water, threatening to shake him loose at any moment. With eyes and mouth shut firmly against the spray of water, Frank hugged the log as tightly as he could. A wind-driven piece of weatherboarding dropped out of the dark sky and slammed into his head, knocking him out. Frank slid slowly off the log and back into the water.

———※———

When the dormitory collapsed Albert had been holding Maggie's hand. The water rushed in, and Maggie was yanked away by the clothesline. Albert was sent through a window and into the water, battered by debris roiling in the whirlpool created by the sinking building. He thrashed under the water, reaching around frantically for Maggie. Finally, running short of breath, he kicked toward the surface. Moments later he emerged from the water, screaming his sister's name.

"Maggie! Maggie!" he wailed, over and over. After a few minutes he saw a large piece of timber floating past and reached out to grab it. His hand landed on Frank's leg.

———※———

Of the sixty-four rooms in Lucas Terrace, only Daisy Thorne's bedroom was left standing, and there was no telling how long it would hold out. The building's east and south wings were utterly destroyed; the parlor in the Thorne apartment had gone down, as had the hallway, Mrs. Thorne's bedroom, and the walls of the floor below. Yet miraculously, Daisy's bedroom perched atop the wreckage, even as the water flowed through the broken window and over the walls of the tiny room, filled to capacity with twenty-two shivering survivors.

The wind and water started ramming the door off of its hinges, prompting Gus, Robert, and Donald Morton to take turns slamming their weight against it to keep the tide out.

Daisy crept over to her bed to be with her mother, aunt, and brother. She reached for their hands and they clasped hers. She then closed her eyes and prayed.

Sam Young held tightly to his door as he sailed on the tide. He whipped his head around madly, fearing that flying debris would catch him unawares. Dead bodies glided by, their cold, wet hands brushing his as the water carried them away. All around he could hear shouts and screams that barely sounded human. Sam struggled to identify landmarks to let him know where he was.

A man sailed past on the current, howling wildly, knocking against him. The rushing water spun Sam around on the door as the terrified man disappeared into the darkness. Then suddenly the screaming stopped. Still trying to steady his raft, Sam knew that the man's life had just ended.

Sam finally got his bearings when he passed the remains of the Garten Verein on Avenue O, four blocks north and four west of where his house had stood. In a few moments he was pushed to the east, and before he knew it, he was at the corner of the Ursuline Convent, trapped in a whirlpool. Along with other city debris— pieces of houses, trash, school desks, clothing, wagon wheels, tree branches, window shutters, mailboxes, books—his door-raft started moving around and around and around, sucked in by the force of the water. But it wasn't the debris that horrified Sam so much as the number of lifeless bodies circling into the whirlpool and crowding around him as he struggled to stay above water.

Overcome at the sight of so much death swirling around him, Sam screamed. There were five, six bodies now, gathering around his raft, and more were entering the whirlpool: men, women, and children, all facedown and stripped of their clothing. Their limbs were stiff, and many had fingers that were gnarled, as if they had been clinging desperately to something that had been torn away from them when they died.

Sam shook his head and wailed as he circled toward the vortex of the whirlpool, together with the gathering corpses, the quick and the dead going around and around together.

———•◦•———

At what remained of Lucas Terrace, there was no screaming. There were only whispered prayers and hushed, clipped conversations. Daisy's bedroom was packed to capacity with the Thornes' neighbors. People huddled on the floor in two feet of water, many shielding their heads. A cluster of men leaned against the door to keep it closed against the tide, but the water still seeped in and flowed over the walls. The Bible that Alice had been reading from now floated at her knees.

Every few minutes more water would surge through the huge gash in the ceiling. People gasped and clung to each other, fearing each wave would bring the fatal blow to Lucas Terrace. The walls continued to shake and groan—cracking and crumbling but refusing to collapse.

Mrs. Hesse, who had been terrified into silence for some time now, fell onto Daisy's bed in a faint, bumping Talia over to the other side. Mr. Hesse and Vernon scurried to help her, fanning her face. Emma and Katherine also moved over to the bed to see what was happening and took the opportunity to sit down. As it was becoming more and more difficult to stand in the shaking room, the bed became a magnet for the other refugees, who were all desperate to escape the freezing-cold water. Alice stood and Daisy helped her lift Talia up to stand with them as the bed was taken over by the others. Daisy held tightly to Talia and Alice, while Danny stood beside her, trying to peek out the window. As the walls rattled harder and harder, it became impossible for Daisy to maintain her grip on her aunt and mother while still clinging to her purse of gold coins. She loosened her grip on the purse and let it fall. The wind quickly whipped it out the window and into the water.

The storm pushed into Daisy's room as the men tried to block its entrance with the door, now completely off its hinges and threatening to fly away. Outside the room pianos and bathtubs bobbed along in the waves as if they were no more than corks.

Her eyes shut tightly, Daisy prayed to herself, her lips trembling as she mouthed words to her Lord. She could feel the grip of Danny's hand on her arm as she held tightly to her mother and aunt. She couldn't bear to open her eyes again and see the agonized expressions on their faces in the moonlight. More than that: Daisy knew she was going to die. And she knew she should continue praying to God, but there was something she couldn't keep from popping into her head: her favorite passage in the book of love letters her fiancé had given her. She had read it over and over earlier that day while the storm, unbeknownst to her at the time, was stirring itself into a killing machine outside. It was a line in a letter Robert Browning wrote to his future wife, Elizabeth Barrett, complimenting her on her poetry—a line that now brought Daisy such calm:

So into me has it gone, and part of me has it become, this great living poetry of yours. . . .

She opened her eyes once more. Daisy thought of Joe, whom she would never see again, and hoped he was safe. Then she closed her eyes again. The wailing wind filled her ears and a new wave sent another deluge into the room as she leaned against the wall and waited for death.

———— ·•· ————

The freezing-cold water brought Frank back to consciousness, and he jerked up his head with a gasp. His leg was still wrapped around the log, and someone had just grabbed it. Frank screamed, and Albert quickly screamed in response, letting go of Frank's leg and plunging back into the water. Frank lost control of the log, slipping completely back into the water and splashing around as he tried to recover his grip. He heaved himself onto the log again, now bleeding from a fresh gash on his forehead.

Albert held on to the log too, though this time he didn't try to pull himself up for fear he would send Frank back into the water. The boys said nothing to each other as they focused single-mindedly on holding on to the log.

Frank looked around for the orphanage. But there was no sign of it; the building had simply disappeared. And where . . . where were the others? No one else was splashing around in the water that he could see. One minute there were ninety children and ten nuns in a building and the next minute there was a terrible void, a silence even more horrifying than the children's wails and screams had been. It was just him and another boy on a log. And . . . who was this boy? Was that Albert . . . with the sister?

"Maggie!" Albert screamed. "Maggie!" He whipped his head around, trying to see something—anything—in the darkness that might suggest the form of his little sister. But there was no answer.

"Maggie!"

Frank couldn't believe that the storm had taken nearly everybody but not him. He thought back to when he left little Tony with Sister Elizabeth so he could run up to the roof. He had intended to come right back down, but. . . . He never saw Tony again. Frank didn't even remember seeing him when he jumped back through the trap door and slid down the ladder. It was so chaotic then. So much noise. Then the boys rushed past him onto the roof. The children were screaming and crying, and even a few of the Sisters looked fearful. Then the floating. And the crash.

Frank and Albert continued clinging to the log as it rode the tide, Frank trying to keep his upper body on top, his arms and legs wrapped around it, and Albert clinging to the side.

"Maggie!"

The full moon was beginning to glimmer through the clouds, making it easy for a delirious Albert to see his sister's golden curls in every tiny sliver of moonlight bouncing on the water.

With his head hanging off the side and half-submerged in the water, Frank suddenly caught a glimpse of something standing up in the water just a few yards away from them. He lifted his head for a better view.

"Look!" he said, pointing in the dark. "Over there!"

Albert followed the direction of Frank's finger with his eyes.

Sticking out of the water—nearly upright—was a tall tree that had been ripped from the ground. The top of the tree bobbed up and down against the lit-up sky.

———·•·———

Sam held on to his door-raft with one hand and tried to paddle his way out of the whirlpool with the other, feeling panic rising as he was jostled among the bodies. Dizzy from traveling around and around, he went back to holding on with both hands. He shut his eyes to concentrate on keeping himself on the slick door, which, he realized with horror, was starting to splinter.

In a few moments, though, the whirlpool had spat him out and pushed him away. Sam now floated on the other side of the Garten Verein, shoved to the northwest by the tide. He could see the roofs of some houses barely sticking out of the water. Many other homes were completely destroyed, just haphazard collections of timber floating among furniture and other decimated buildings. Sam saw no electric lights anywhere and heard no human voices.

I am the only one left, he thought, sailing through the moonlit night. *It is just me.*

Then he heard a sound behind him, piercing through the roar of wind. It was a woman crying for help somewhere in the distance. Sam wondered how far away she was as the tide pushed him farther to the north. Another person ... alive. Surely he should try to find her? Turn his raft around and follow the sound of her voice ... but that would be impossible. He would have to swim against the tide. He would exhaust himself trying to find her and what good would he be to her if he did?

He had to take care of himself now. The storm had spared him so far. He had taken a brutal beating, yes. His house was gone. And all that stood between him and a drowning death was this increasingly battered balcony door.

Sam tried to block out the sound of the woman's cries as they slipped farther into the distance. There was nothing he could do, he told himself. The wind carried him away, and for the first time since he'd been riding on the tide, he wished it would carry him faster.

Daisy's eyes were still shut tight. The wind still battered her bedroom, and the water still flowed over the walls. She had made her peace with God and was ready to go; she hoped only that her end would be quick and painless. The room was filled with the sounds of the wind and rain and lit dimly by the full moon behind the clouds; the twenty-two people huddling there, waiting to die, had fallen silent.

It shocked Daisy, then, when Gus, who moments before had been helping to keep the door standing against the incoming water, tugged on her arm and called her name.

"Miss Daisy! Miss Daisy!" he said. Daisy opened her eyes and saw Gus leaning toward her, though she couldn't see his smile.

"What is it?" she whispered, her voice buried deep in her throat.

"Please, take my hand," Gus said.

Daisy slowly came back to herself and looked first at her mother and then at her aunt Talia, whose hands she had been holding tightly. They each loosened their grip.

"Please," he repeated.

Daisy gave him her hand and he led her a few feet over to the window, where he nudged a few people out of the way so she could get an unobstructed view. The moon was high in the sky, and it cast a glow upon the water and the remnants of the flooded city.

"Look," he said, angling his arm toward the top of the window and pointing.

After a few moments of searching for what he was pointing to, Daisy shook her head.

"I'm sorry, I don't know what . . ."

Realizing the difference between his height and hers, Gus held out his hands, threaded his fingers together, and said, "Up you go."

Daisy looked at him like he was crazy, but something about his friendly yet forceful demeanor inspired her to obey. She placed her foot in his hands, and he lifted her up so she could get a better view.

"You're the bravest person I've ever known," he said. "I wanted you to see this first."

Daisy gazed intently out at the water. All of a sudden, she realized what he had been pointing to.

The salt cedar trees. She could see their slender, naked branches—usually dense with gray-green foliage—poking above the waterline. Just a little while ago, the trees had been completely submerged by the Gulf, nowhere to be seen. Now here they were, visible again.

The water was receding.

8

A THOUSAND NEEDLES

FRANK WATCHED THE PARTIALLY UPROOTED tree as it bobbed and swayed on the tide.

"Hey, now, hang onto this stupid log!" an out-of-breath Frank said to Albert as they held on to the same piece of timber. "We should swim to that tree."

Albert was silent.

"Hey, buddy, can you swim?" Frank asked.

The tree wasn't too far, but it looked like it was floating away from them.

Albert put his head down on the log and gripped it tightly.

"Buddy! Hey! You hear me? Come on, see how big it is? And we can probably climb up and get out of the water."

Albert said nothing.

Frank's side of the log started to come apart. He watched as the distance between the boys and the tree grew. The rain seemed to let up before returning a few seconds later in full force.

"I'm tellin' ya, we gotta go!" Frank was shouting now. "Gotta get to the tree!"

But Albert was frozen with his limbs wrapped around the log. He didn't think he could move even if he wanted to.

"Oh, hang it!" Frank yelped. He slipped into the water and started swimming. Albert lifted his head and watched as Frank swam fast to the tree, leaving him behind. In under a minute Frank reached the tree and grabbed onto its trunk. He clambered up the tree as it bobbed on the tide, carefully making his way up to the lowest branches. He straddled one branch about three feet above the water and looked back over at Albert. "Come on!"

Albert looked at Frank sitting there in the tree, his silhouette against the sky both frightening and fantastic. The sight stirred Albert to action, and before he could tell himself no, he had unwrapped himself from the log and started swimming. Every muscle in his body ached as he forced himself through the water, and he could taste his own blood being washed into his mouth. Finally he made it to the tree and hoisted himself onto the trunk. When he did this, the top half of the tree where Frank sat tipped down toward the water, and Frank yelped, "Careful!"

Albert steadied himself and crept cautiously up the trunk toward the branches. He straddled a branch opposite Frank and looked out over the water for his sister. The tree returned to its almost vertical position in the water.

From their perches in the tree, the boys took in a broad view of the devastated city. They had been carried two miles into the Gulf of Mexico, and they could see that Galveston had been almost completely swallowed up by the storm. Far in the distance they saw the roofs of buildings and houses poking out above the waterline. Everything else was submerged.

"Maggie!" Albert shouted, looking around. It was no use. If she was out there, how could she even hear him above this wind?

The boys had to hold on tightly as the tree bobbed on the water, the top swinging back and forth as the wind curled through its branches. Frank lowered his head. What were they going to do now? The orphanage was gone. The Sisters were gone. Their city was gone. Where were they supposed to go? And how do you get anywhere floating on a tree?

Frank jerked his head up suddenly. He peered down at the roots of the tree—ripped from the ground, they now dangled just below the waterline. There was something tangled in them.

Looking down at the bottom of the tree, Frank could make out the shape of something caught in the tangle of roots at the surface of the water. He wiped his eyes and leaned down to get a better look.

No, it wasn't some*thing*, it was some*one*.

William.

———————◆◆———————

The screaming didn't stop. It grew. It was everywhere, surrounding Sam on all sides and making escape impossible. The woman he'd heard earlier had been joined by yelps and howls from others here, there, and everywhere—all anonymous, faceless voices on the air. But Sam couldn't see anyone. And what could he do if he could see them? All he had was this door he'd pulled off his house and even that was crumbling beneath him.

The current had pushed Sam northwest of the whirlpool he'd been trapped in near the Ursuline Convent. The rain pelted him as he gripped his raft tighter and tighter. He couldn't believe how quickly he had been carried across town. With one final push his raft was sent into a pile of debris in the middle of Thirty-Fourth Street at M½, fifteen blocks from where he had originally started. For the first time in what seemed like hours, he was able to gain a steady footing on a pile of crushed houses, furniture, trees, wagons, and other rubble. Still holding on to the raft, he dug his feet into the pile to get a foothold as the current helpfully pressed him into it.

He realized that he didn't hear the screaming anymore. He could not hear a single human voice. Had he imagined it all? Had it been a trick of the wind, its voice mimicking the terrified shouts and cries of men, women, and children?

The raindrops pricked his skin and the wind tossed bucketsful of water in his face as he tried to steady himself against the mound of debris. Suddenly the door that he had been using as a raft broke apart in his hands, and he was forced to make a grab for the pile itself.

His hand slammed onto a nail protruding from a piece of wood. He shouted in pain, blood spilling from his wounded hand. He heard his scream echo through the night, and he grabbed desperately for a beam sticking out of the mound. Finally he was able to steady himself once again, though his hand throbbed with pain.

Then he heard a single, solitary scream.

"Help me! Help me!"

It was a woman's voice. And she was very close.

———◦◦◦———

A cat's raspy meow echoed around the ruins of Lucas Terrace. The sound, an invisible sign of life, brought the refugees hunkered down inside Daisy Thorne's bedroom back to themselves. Eyes opened for the first time in many minutes, and chattering began to cut through the sound of the storm.

It was still dark, and the rain and wind continued, but less violently. None of the cats had been heard from since before the parlor fell, so it was a surprise to hear such a sound puncturing the air. For the first time in many hours, the sound of a single crying cat brought comfort to the refugees, rather than annoyance. Perhaps life would go on, after all.

Daisy peered out the window to look around. The full moon's rays poked through the rain clouds and reflected dimly on the water. There was debris everywhere and not a standing house in sight. All around her, proof of the city's utter destruction was slowly emerging from the receding water. To the east the salt cedar trees continued to materialize from the Gulf. And now a cat's meowing. Could it be that the storm was over?

Daisy carefully stepped off the window ledge and onto the floor. She walked lightly around the room, following the cat's meow but unable to find it in the darkness.

"Daisy," Alice whispered as the room shook. "Be careful, darling. We should stay still."

Daisy's mother was right. Who knew what state the building was in? Daisy's bedroom could be poised to collapse into the water, needing only one false move by someone inside.

Daisy returned to the window where she watched the scene intently for changes to the landscape. She was wet and freezing. She had lost her shoes, her clothes were soaked, and her hair was plastered to her head and down her shoulders.

More lonely meowing filled the room. Daisy crept back to where her mother and aunt stood, and where Danny was curled up on the floor, hugging his knees. She grabbed Aunt Talia's hand.

"Auntie, I think the storm might be on its way out."

Talia gasped and squeezed Daisy's hand. The room continued to shake in the wind, and the floorboards and walls creaked. Gus stepped forward gently and tapped Daisy on the shoulder.

"Miss Daisy, we need to get out of this room. It's not safe to be here now."

Daisy looked at Gus and then around the room at the dark faces looking at her expectantly.

"Leave?" she said.

"Yes," Gus replied. He pointed up to the top of one of the walls. With no ceiling to prop it up, Daisy's bedroom wall was leaning down, threatening to flatten everyone inside.

"All of us. Now."

"Hey! Hey!" Frank yelled down at William from the branch he straddled at the top of the tree. Then he called to Albert. "What's his name, do you know?"

Albert shook his head.

Then Frank recalled Joseph, whom he had comforted earlier in the day. Joseph had an older brother . . . what was his name? "Will! William!"

Down below, lying in the tangle of roots that stretched below the water, William stirred. He had cuts on his head, and his shirt was gone, revealing more scratches and cuts on his arms and torso.

"Up here! Up here!"

William opened his eyes and saw the blurry image of Frank above him waving his hands. His eyes slowly began to focus, and his ears, now sufficiently drained of water, started picking up sounds more clearly. He jerked upward, suddenly remembering what had happened.

"Joseph! Where are you! I can't see you!" he shouted.

Shivering and breathless, he lifted himself up and began

trying to crawl up the tree trunk. But he overestimated his strength and quickly fell back into the water.

From his perch three feet above, Frank lifted his legs, grabbed the branch with his hands, and swung around so that he hung from it, with his feet hovering just a few inches above the water. After a few seconds he let go and dropped into the water.

Albert looked down as the boys splashed and thrashed under the water, Frank trying to get a hold of William and pull him up onto the tree as a shell-shocked William resisted. Frank grabbed William around the neck, pulled him over to the tree and, with all the strength he could summon, hoisted him onto the base where the roots began to fan out. He then pulled himself up and flopped down next to William, out of breath.

The tree swayed back and forth like a metronome. Albert clung to his branch more tightly, afraid that any minute the wind would either switch direction or regain its strength and send him flying.

"Let's get outta this water," Frank said, lifting himself up. Standing precariously on the gnarled platform of roots, Frank held his hand out toward William, who slowly got to his feet. They began climbing back up the swinging tree, the glow from the full moon, now more visible in the sky, lighting their way.

A single bare foot poked out the window at the Lucas Terrace. It was Daisy's. She had decided—against the wishes of her mother, her aunt, and Gus—that she should be the first to go outside and see if it was safe. The rain was still coming down and the wind still whipping, but more lightly, more fitfully than before. More and more it seemed as if the monster had done its worst to Galveston and had moved on to another town.

Daisy carefully placed her foot on a plank of wood at the top of a wet pile of rubble. She expected that it would shake or give way when she put the weight of both of her feet on it, but to her surprise it stayed firmly in place, packed alongside other pieces of material that just hours ago had composed homes, churches, stores, and schools. She gingerly walked around, surprised that the rubble was so sturdy under her feet.

She looked around. Galveston was gone. Daisy looked for signs of life anywhere around Lucas Terrace and saw no one. Suddenly she heard the walls of her bedroom creak again and saw a piece of plaster crumble and spit dust onto the debris. She returned to the window.

"It's safe, I think," she said to Gus. "We should start helping people out."

The refugees began carefully climbing through the window. Daisy helped them out and directed them to sit down on the wreckage.

"Be careful, Mrs. Hesse, don't go too far down. The water is still very high."

Daisy helped Alice, Talia, and Danny make their way out. She settled them on a pile of rubble jutting out into the water on the east side, where they could watch the salt cedar trees as they slowly reappeared in the distance.

Returning to the window, Daisy gazed down at something floating past below. She shuddered.

A grisly parade of naked bodies swirled into view on the current. The hands of two of them, a man and a woman, were clasped together as they floated lifelessly in the moonlight.

———

Sam had never been so cold in his life. Most of his clothes

had been stripped from his body, and the rain, though it continued to let up, still fell from the sky in light sheets as the storm exited the city. He sat shivering at the top of the debris pile, his body covered with cuts and bruises, his hand still spilling blood. Adding to his misery was the shrill screeching of a woman floating somewhere near him in the darkness, filling the air with a horrific echo it was impossible to ignore or escape.

The last thing Sam wanted to do was get back in the water. That would be crazy. But oh, the screaming. If only he had the strength to face that water again, to dive back in and swim against the tide to track down the source of the screams. But he was too tired for that now. There was nothing he could do.

He clambered to his feet atop the mass of debris and,

The aftermath of the storm: a view of the Gulf of Mexico from where Galveston once stood

standing in his underwear, looked around for signs of life, ducking and shielding his head from the stray objects still flying through the air. He quickly stooped back down to sit, afraid of losing his balance and being cast back into the tide.

Sam shivered as he curled up to rest in the remains of a wagon seat that had imbedded itself at the top of the pile of rubble. He winced every time he heard the woman scream for help. He closed his eyes tightly and wrapped his arms around himself, moving his shaking hands up and down his arms in a desperate attempt to create some warmth. Suddenly the rain began falling harder and the wind regained momentum, as if the storm were bent on taking one final jab at the surviving citizens of Galveston.

The raindrops felt like a thousand needles landing on Sam's skin, and he yelled out, writhing in agony on the wagon seat.

Mercifully, the resurgence didn't last. The rain slackened and the wind, though still intense, was just an echo of what it had been only thirty minutes before.

Facedown on the wagon seat, Sam prayed for the rain to stop. As the storm continued to die down, Sam realized something. He rolled over onto the wreckage and sat up. He could no longer hear the woman screaming.

He looked around for any changes to the scenery in front of him. Soon enough, he saw a body float into view.

It was the figure of a woman. Like Sam's, her clothes had been ripped from her body, and she was clad only in her underclothes. She floated on her stomach, her head submerged. Though he couldn't be sure it was the woman whose screams had so unsettled him, he had a strong feeling that it was.

The body drifted closer and closer to the debris pile. A small wave rammed the body up against the pile, and the flowing water turned it over and over. Then Sam understood exactly what had stopped the woman's screams.

Her head wasn't submerged. It was gone.

9

THE GOLDEN CITY

THE FAINT MOONLIGHT SHONE DOWN on the tree as it dipped and swayed on the water. Frank, William, and Albert each clung to a different branch. For an hour they floated in the Gulf as the wind and rain eased but did not stop. There was a glow on the surface of the water, the light creating tiny radiant curves and golden water droplets that bounced around on the gleaming surface.

A near-delirious William clung to his branch, his arms wrapped around it, his head twitching, and his eyes half open. A riot of noises echoed in his head: the clanging of machinery, the ringing of church bells, the buzzing of telephones, the clomping of horse hooves on the streets, and the screech of streetcars as they bounded along their tracks.

William raised his head, his eyes glassy. "Hey! Do you hear that?"

"What?" Frank asked.

"The noises . . ."

Frank turned to Albert, who was slumped on his branch and hugging the trunk of the tree with both arms.

"Do you hear anything, buddy?" Frank asked him. Albert shook his head and rubbed his eyes.

"Yeah, I don't hear nothing but that dang wind," Frank said. He looked back over at Albert again and saw that he was now sitting straight up, his eyes wide, and pointing to something down in the water.

William's eyes opened wide for the first time since he landed on the tree. In an instant the noises ringing in his ears were gone. All he heard was the fierce wind and rain. But he saw what Albert was pointing at. Frank looked into the water and he could see it too.

It was one of the bedrooms at the orphanage, lit by the moonlight, undamaged by the storm. And there were Sister Elizabeth and Sister Vincent leaning down and kissing the children as they tucked them into bed.

———•◆•———

Sam sat dazed atop the debris pile and watched the water level go down, revealing more and more of the wrecked city underneath. The city emerged looking like it had been chewed up and spat out by an angry sea-monster.

Summoning all of his strength, Sam began climbing down to the street. He shivered uncontrollably as he stepped into the water once again, dreading the feel of it against his skin. The ice-cold water was up to his chest. He looked around him, trying to get his bearings. *Where am I?* he thought. At first he could detect no recognizable landmark among the wreckage. Then he saw it.

A little elevated cottage, half a block from where he stood. It was beaten and battered, but it was still standing. Sam took a step toward it and the hard chill of the water shot through him like an electric shock. The cold was unbearable, and his body was so weak that he feared he would collapse and sink if he dared take another step. And the water level was slowly but steadily falling, leaving Sam more exposed to the cold wind and the prickly rain. But he couldn't just stay where he was—he'd either freeze to death or faint and drown.

So Sam willed his body into action. He took another step and winced, shivering. Then another. And another. Slowly he bridged the distance between the debris pile and the cottage that he hoped might deliver him from the deathly chill of the water.

As he approached he thought he could hear chattering voices coming from inside the cottage. Or was it just the staccato beat of the wind against the side of the house? He finally reached the steps to the porch, which was now above the waterline, and he instinctively lifted his foot to meet the stairs that should have been there. But the steps had been washed away by the storm, and Sam's foot had nothing to step onto.

He lost his balance and fell face first onto the edge of the porch. His bruised and bloodied body looked like just another corpse.

Streetcars ran on tracks in the moonlight. People walked on sidewalks and stopped to look into shop windows, chatting to each other with wide grins on their faces. Vegetable sellers shouted out their offerings, and the sounds of carnival rides on the beach rang out. There was no hurricane. No rain, no wind. Galveston wasn't destroyed, it was right there, at the bottom of the tree. Frank, Albert, and William all saw it.

The boys were mesmerized. Their nightmare was over, it seemed. No. Their nightmare had never happened.

The dormitories stood once again on the beach. William looked for his brother, Mother Camillus, Henry, and the Sisters. He looked around for his friends among the dunes and salt cedar trees. He looked at the empty stable. "Where are the horses?" he asked the others.

Frank squinted into the water, trying to get a glimpse of Saint Mary's Infirmary. He knew it was down there somewhere amid the trolleys and churches, the restaurants and bustling streets.

Albert saw it all too. But he also saw something that William and Frank didn't. Standing on the beach, her blond curls bouncing in the breeze, was Maggie. Her icy blue eyes stared directly at him. She waved.

Not taking his eyes off of his sister, Albert scooted back toward the trunk of the tree, turned and grabbed it, and swung his legs around. He lowered himself slowly toward the water, eager to join his sister in the golden city. As he came closer, he saw Maggie's mouth move, but he couldn't hear what she was saying to him.

"What? Maggie, what?" he shouted.

Maggie didn't answer. She just stood on the beach, looking sweetly at him and giggling.

Albert lowered a foot down to join Maggie on the beach. But instead of touching solid ground, Albert was stunned to find himself dipping his toes into cold water. Maggie's face dissolved into ripples in the glimmering Gulf.

Albert looked up at Frank and William, whose faces were white with shock. He looked back down and saw that the golden city had disappeared.

———— • • ————

Daisy wiped her forehead with the back of her hand, staring out at the devastated city emerging around her. Her clothes clung tightly to her body, and she was covered in lime and mortar from the falling walls. She leaned down and pulled a large piece of fabric from the ruins and draped it over her shoulders. Looking down at how awkwardly it covered her, she realized it was a sopping wet piece of the dining room rug.

Outside her bedroom Daisy felt exposed to the chill of the wind and the drizzling rain. She picked her way carefully over the rubble to check on her mother, aunt, and brother, who were all sitting on the remains of Lucas Terrace's brick façade, which now stood only three feet above the ground.

Danny sat next to Alice, leaning his head on her chest as she stroked it, while Talia sat covering her head with her hands, shivering and quietly crying. Daisy knelt down and rubbed Talia's back.

"Auntie, please don't cry," Daisy said. "We're OK now. We've got to thank God for that. Here." Daisy pulled the piece of rug from her shoulders and carefully draped it over her aunt's, careful not to allow the rough and soggy material to brush against the back of Talia's neck. Talia took her hands from her head and held the carpet against her, desperate for some covering.

Daisy sat beside Talia and put her arm around her. "Look at the salt cedars," she said. Talia lifted her head and gazed out

In the days after the storm, a relief party looks for survivors

toward where the salt cedar trees reached their branches out of the water and pointed toward the early-morning sky.

A high-pitched sound pierced through the muffled echo of the dying storm. Talia jerked her head up immediately and she looked over at Daisy with excited eyes. Daisy smiled at Talia.

"Jasper."

———

The door to the cottage opened, and two black gentlemen, clad only in wet undershorts, quietly crept onto the porch and approached Sam's body. One of the men, Leonard Johnson, knelt down and placed his hand on the side of Sam's neck.

"Is he dead, Lennie?" the other man, Jerome Serkus, asked. Leonard looked over at Jerome with a surprised expression on his face.

"Lord knows he looks it," he said. "But I think he's still with us."

Sam suddenly shook with cold, startling the two men. Leonard and Jerry took Sam in their arms, lifted him up, and carried him inside. Sam moaned and his eyes rolled to the back of his head as his feet dragged along the porch. The two men carried Sam inside to the larger of the cottage's two rooms, where a total of eighteen other Galvestonians had been waiting out the storm.

The darkened room was strewn with broken, waterlogged furniture and cracked pictures in broken frames. The wooden floors were a craggy mountain range of warped and twisted paneling. Leonard and Jerry carried Sam over to what was left of the stained and ripped-up couch, which slumped onto the wet floor.

Sam's arrival sparked a flurry of activity among the people in the room. They seemed to forget their misery in their eagerness to aid the new guest, who seemed very near death.

Sam's eyes fluttered open as the refugees in the room gathered around the couch to help him. Two women helped position Sam on the couch. A few men stripped off their wet shirts and wrapped them around Sam's shoulders and torso to provide him some warmth. A young boy in a cloth cap and bare feet stood next to where Sam laid his head. Looking into Sam's glassy eyes, the boy pulled his cap off his head and secured it onto Sam's.

Leonard walked over to the front door to see how things looked outside.

The sun was rising, casting its golden beams over the draining, wounded city. Leonard opened the door wide.

———◆◆◆———

A ray of light shot up from the horizon as Frank, Albert, and William, dazed, clung to their branches. The emerging daylight confirmed what the boys had by now figured out: what they had been looking at was just an illusion—a mirage that, remarkably, they'd all experienced together. They hadn't really seen the people of Galveston walking through town. There were no more streetcars zipping through the streets. The Sisters of Charity, and their family and friends at the orphanage—Maggie, Joseph, Mother Camillus, Henry, everyone—were all gone. Swallowed up by the sea.

The boys were adrift several miles into the Gulf. Though the storm had passed far inland by now and the water level in the city was draining away, the three orphans were far away from the wreckage, without the strength to navigate back home. And where was home now, anyway?

An oppressive silence filled the air that had for so long been filled with the sounds of the storm. Frank looked at his fellow survivors—thanks to the daylight, he got a good look at their injuries for the first time. Both William and Albert were covered with cuts and bruises, and their hair was matted with blood. Their clothes had been stripped away and both clung to their branches wearing only their underwear. Their bare skin was torn up, as though they'd been attacked by savage animals. Frank's own head throbbed from a blow he'd received during the surge. He gently touched his head where it hurt, and he shuddered. Looking over at Albert, Frank realized he didn't know his name.

Galveston residents pick through wreckage in the days after the storm

"Hey, buddy," Frank called after Albert. But Albert didn't lift his head.

"Buddy! What's your name?"

Albert's eyes were open, but he didn't speak.

Frank looked over at William, who was staring out to sea. Without turning his head, William said to Frank, "His name is Albert. Maggie was his sister."

Frank nodded. His eyes followed William's gaze.

In the distance something dark gray moved on the water,

coming into view. It came closer, its contours becoming more and more visible against the pale sky. It was massive.

"Is that a building?" Frank asked, dumbfounded. "Is that Galveston?"

William looked at Frank with uncertainty, wondering if he could trust his own eyes.

"No, that's not a building. It's a ship."

———◆———

Daisy scaled the pile of remains once again, following the sound of Jasper's crying. She knelt down and peeked into the cavity between her bedroom and the rubble-filled floor below, thinking that Jasper had likely crept into a hard-to-reach area that she would have to coax him out of.

"Jasper! Jasper, honey!" Jasper answered with a muffled mew. He didn't appear to be under her room. She stood and walked around to the window of her bedroom. Jasper mewed again, and Daisy realized he was inside. She climbed through the open window and carefully stepped inside, yelling Jasper's name excitedly.

He answered again, a muffled whimper this time. She was very close to him. She looked under the bed and under the bedside table before hearing another cry, this one definitely coming from the wardrobe on the other side of the bed. Daisy scuttled over to the wardrobe and flung open the two doors, fully expecting that Jasper would come flying out with claws bared and ready to scratch. But there was no Jasper to be seen among the stacks of folded, soggy clothes and hung-up dresses. Jasper mewed again.

Daisy looked down and saw two glowing green eyes staring at her from the slit between the main shelf of the wardrobe and the drawer underneath it. Daisy pulled open the drawer, excitedly screamed Jasper's name and picked him up, and promptly received a scratch on her cheek.

"Hey! Someone gimme some help up here!" Gus shouted from his position on the wreckage next to Daisy's room. "I hear someone!"

Daisy climbed out the window and put Jasper down, and Robert hiked back up from street-level to help.

Gus pointed to the area directly under Daisy's bedroom, completely packed with rubble. "There's someone down in there. Alive. You hear that?"

A gasping sound came from below. The gasping turned to gurgling. It sounded very far away.

"How can we even get to them?" Daisy said.

Gus removed some pieces of wood and concrete, trying to clear a path, but every time he tried to move something, it sent several other pieces of debris cascading down. A piece of siding slammed against Robert's leg and he bent over in pain. Gus stopped moving, afraid that he would set the whole pile loose and create an avalanche.

Every few seconds another gurgle sounded from below.

"The entire first floor . . . ," he said. "It's just packed with all of . . . *this*." He reached his arm out and gestured toward the pieces of the collapsed building. "How can we even . . . ?"

"It's impossible," Robert answered, shaking his head.

A whimper could be heard below. It continued for a few seconds before giving way to a desperate gasp for air. Then silence.

Daisy looked at Gus and Robert. The men hung their heads and started climbing down to the street.

10

DAYLIGHT

As the water receded Galveston began to stir. Dazed survivors emerged from their hiding places, picking their way through the wreckage of their homes. The Gulf and bay waters had largely drained out of the city, though large pockets of slimy water still dotted the landscape. The sad and desperate search for family and friends began.

All communication between Galveston and the outside world had been cut. There was no bridge to the mainland. The storm survivors were trapped on an island of corpses.

Dead bodies were everywhere, many mutilated by the objects that killed them—the slates of roofs, telephone poles, slabs of concrete, wagon wheels. The remains of whole families lay scattered in their yards, houses collapsed around and on top of them. In death, fathers clung to fallen timbers; children clutched mothers' skirts; young girls clasped brothers in their arms; mothers hugged babies to their chests.

The sun rose over a city of the dead.

Two sailors rowed in a small boat that had been dispatched from a Navy ship patrolling the Gulf of Mexico. The water was calm, and they were cutting through it swiftly toward their destination, the floating tree.

Frank kept absently touching the wounds on his head. Albert clung to his branch with his head down. William, perched on a branch that stretched out in the direction of the approaching boat, stared squarely at the sailors as they rowed toward the boys.

"Hallo! You boys! You all right? If you can understand me, wave a hand!"

Frank, Albert, and William all looked at the sailors gliding toward them in the boat and each raised a scraped and bloodied hand. They understood.

Storm refugees filled the wounded St. Mary's Infirmary on the northeastern stretch of the island. Two buildings on the grounds of the hospital had collapsed, the chapel next to them had been warped and hollowed out by the wind, almost every window in the two brick structures making up the main part of the infirmary had been shattered, and part of the roof of a newly built annex had blown away.

Still, the Sisters at St. Mary's had work to do, caring for the many unfortunates who had shown up at the infirmary's doorstep during the storm. Overseeing the treatment of refugees and organizing the Sisters were Mother Mechtilde and her assistant superior, Mother Gabriel. In the early morning, as the sun rose, Mother Mechtilde spoke to Zachary Scott, a seventeen-year-old medical student who was helping to treat the injured.

"Young Zachary," Mother Mechtilde said, "we must ask that you take a trip for us."

Zachary nodded and wiped the blood from his hands with a towel.

"We are all dreadfully worried about the orphanage. You must go there and report back what you find. As quickly as you can."

He nodded again and turned to leave.

One of the hurricane's eight thousand victims, underneath the remains of the wharf

"Zachary . . . ," Mother Mechtilde said, but then couldn't bring herself to speak the next words. After a few moments, she continued. "May God go with you."

Zachary ventured out of the infirmary.

To herself, Mother Mechtilde whispered, "God help us all."

———————

Sam awoke on a broken couch. He opened his eyes and squinted into a bright morning. The blinding whiteness was finally eclipsed by the form of Leonard.

"Sir. Sir?" He spoke softly, nudging Sam in the arm.

Sam's eyes opened wider to look at Leonard, whose head was outlined by the golden glow of the sunlight shining behind him into the cottage.

"Charlie?" Sam whispered.

"No, sir." Leonard smiled. "No, sir. Name's Leonard. What's yours?"

Sam was quiet for a moment, his breathing labored and raspy.

"Sam Young."

"It's nice to meet you, Mr. Young," Leonard said. "Say, Mr. Young, some of us are gonna go outside, try to see . . . what we can see. And try to find a way to get downtown."

Sam slowly lifted himself up on his elbows and looked around the room. The front door was wide open, and he could hear voices outside the cottage. Children were running in and out. He could feel himself coming back to life; the blood was quickening in his veins, and his heart thumped excitedly in his chest.

"I'll go with you."

"Are you sure, Mr. Young? You look awfully weak. . . ."

But Sam was already sitting up and swinging his bleeding, swollen feet onto the floor. He let out a gravelly cough and then cleared his throat.

"Help me to my feet, would you, Leonard, my good man?"

———•-•-•———

Zachary rode along the beach on a borrowed horse. After leaving St. Mary's he had gone directly down Eighth Street to the home of Mr. Levy, the undertaker. He knew Levy had a horse and hoped to borrow it—assuming it survived.

When he reached the house, which was damaged but still in one piece, the horse was standing in the front, surrounded by debris from the neighboring yards. Curiously, the horse was not tethered to anything. Zachary soon understood why: she was trapped in the yard, hemmed in by wreckage on all sides.

After getting permission from Mr. Levy to take the horse, Zachary spent a few minutes clearing a narrow pathway through the debris. He hopped on the horse and led her on a zigzagging path, southward through the slimy and cluttered streets. He hoped to get to the shoreline as quickly as possible because then it would be a straight shot to the orphanage.

It took Zachary an hour to travel the three miles along a devastated shoreline. He felt dizzy from the sight of so much destruction and death—piles of bodies on the beach, hundreds of corpses floating in the water, miles of housing reduced to an endless landscape of shattered timber and mortar. And the smell—he'd never encountered such a horrible stench. It seemed to be offending even the horse, who irritably bobbed its head from side to side and was clearly getting tired.

Zachary pulled on the horse's reins. They had arrived at the place where the orphanage's two dormitories should have been standing, behind the resilient salt cedar trees. But there was nothing there. Nothing.

Zachary circled the grounds over and over, looking for any traces of the Sisters of Charity buildings. There was not a single piece of timber, not even an outline on the ground suggesting what had once stood there.

This couldn't be. The orphans and nuns had to be somewhere. But where could they have gone? There were no buildings standing for miles. There was just this mangled beach. This beach . . .

Suddenly Zachary felt a welling-up inside him—thoughts of the many bloated bodies he'd seen on his long ride mixed with the stunning disappearance of the orphanage. No bodies. Nothing. He jumped off the horse and got sick on the sand. Finally, breathing heavily, with his head throbbing, he got back on the horse.

Zachary nudged the horse forward and headed back to town, his heart heavy, his face the color of ash.

Outside her bedroom, Daisy stood on the top of the debris pile, her face bleeding once again. She turned and looked down at her mother, brother, and aunt, all of whom now stood on the litter-strewn street. She watched as Jasper quickly hopscotched his way down the mound of concrete, brick, mortar, timber, and furniture crushed beneath Daisy's bedroom. Reaching the street, the cat rushed up to Talia and rubbed himself against her tired legs.

Daisy remained on the debris pile. Gazing over what remained of Lucas Terrace, her eyes fell on something that sent a chill up her spine. But she gave no indication that she had seen anything. Instead, she silently and carefully climbed down the pile to rejoin her family. Reaching the street, she hugged her mother and turned around to look at what was left of their home. She looked from Danny to Talia and back to her mother, all of them exhausted and shaken, but with a new and strange sensation of having defied death, together. Daisy decided not to ruin the moment by revealing what she had seen in the ruins. And anyway, everyone already knew that Mrs. McCauley was dead.

There's a big difference, though, Daisy thought, *between knowing something was true and seeing an actual body twisted, crushed, and hanging off of her mother's bed under multiple stories of rubble.* She knew that she would be haunted by that image whenever she closed her eyes.

The boat was more comfortable than the tree, that was for sure, Frank thought as he, William, Albert, and the two sailors steered toward Fort Crockett in the rowboat. The air was completely still, with no wind to push the boat along, so the sailors had their work cut out for them to get the boat to Galveston's Gulf shore.

The sailors had brought blankets from the ship, so all three boys were now wrapped up and dry for the first time in more than a day.

The sailors had no sooner covered William and Albert with the blankets than the two boys settled themselves on the floor of the boat and fell asleep. Frank, wrapped in his own blanket, looked down at them and then touched the wounds on his own head again, flinching at the pain.

In the daylight Frank looked ravaged: his hair was caked with blood, streams of it still trailing down to his ears; his lips were slashed and scabbed over; his eyes were sunken into their sockets and encircled by grayish blue rings.

The only sound Frank could hear was the steady knocking of the oars dipping into the water, pivoting around and against the side of the boat, then back into the water again.

Frank watched as more and more of Galveston became visible from the boat. He had never seen the city from this distance, but, still, he knew it didn't look right. The view he had now was of a city blown to pieces. He turned to one of the sailors. "Mister, you think we'll be to land soon?"

The only house left standing on Galveston's miles of beach

"I reckon so, Frank. Just a little ways to go now. Why don't you lie down and give your eyes a little rest, huh, buddy?"

But Frank couldn't possibly shut his eyes. The sun was too bright.

———•◦•———

Sam and Jerry sat in the back of a wagon as it slowly made its way downtown. Leonard sat in the front, holding the reins and trying to navigate his horse through streets littered with sludge, debris, and corpses. Every few minutes, it seemed, Leonard had to stop the wagon and enlist Jerry's help to remove an obstacle from the wagon's path.

The wagon was the only one Sam could see that was headed into town. All other wagons they passed were moving south toward the Gulf. And they were all filled to the top with piles of dead bodies. Men, women, children. Flopped on top of each other like sacks of grain.

So many bodies lay exposed in the quickly rising heat that survivors began to fear the risk of contamination. Just after dawn wagons loaded up with corpses had begun to cut a path to the Gulf shore through the putrid slime and muck left behind by the receding water. The bodies were to be loaded onto barges and taken out to be dumped into the sea.

Sam watched scenes of desperation and death unfold as the wagon pushed through town. A young couple searched for their two missing children. A little boy stood over the dead bodies of his parents and siblings. A woman held just the limbs of what had once been her baby.

Sam and Jerry held their noses. The stench of the dead was already filling the city.

Sam wanted to shut his eyes but he couldn't. He felt he had some sort of obligation to witness the horror that he had survived.

The wagon turned on Broadway and headed east. The street was a confusing tangle of uprooted trees, shattered houses with their contents spilled out, and bodies everywhere. Piles of human corpses lay in heaps alongside dead horses, dogs, cats, chickens, and other animals, as well as rotting vegetation, furniture, and every other conceivable item a household might have safely held the day before. Sam's wagon passed by groups of men with pursed lips, grimly loading more wagons with more bodies to be carried to the sea. After struggling a few blocks along the mucky, carcass-strewn street, Sam had finally seen enough. A moan pierced the air, and Sam looked over to see an old woman on her knees beating on the chest of her dead son, who lay naked in the soggy grass.

Sam lay down in the wagon and closed his eyes. He then pressed his arm against his face to block out the stench of death.

———————

Daisy sat at a small table in a bedroom in the house of Bill and Margaret Tartt and wept.

The Tartts' house had experienced water damage and broken windows, but it was still standing. It was now a haven for storm refugees who had nowhere to go. Daisy would share a room with her mother, and Talia and Danny were down the hall.

Jasper meowed and rubbed against Daisy's legs while she cried. It was the first time she'd allowed herself to cry since the storm began. But she cried for only a minute. She reminded herself that she was one of the lucky ones.

Daisy wiped her eyes and picked up her pen. She was

After the storm bodies were gathered up in wagons all over Galveston

writing a letter she hoped to send her fiancé as soon as communication to the mainland was restored. Until she could send the letter, she resolved to just keep on writing it.

"In truth, dearest Joseph, I feel like I have been given a marvelous blessing. To have been brought so close to the infinite and to see how small finite things are."

Daisy thought of Mr. and Mrs. McCauley, and the way they spent their last moments. Together, in a strange room, declaring their love to each other. She tried to get the image of Mrs. McCauley's dead body out of her head.

Daisy stopped writing again because the words were beginning to swim in front of her.

It took Zachary three hours to get back to St. Mary's from where the orphanage had once stood. Along the beach he passed numerous pyres, their flames rising high, smoke curling in a dark plume in the sky over the beach. Survivors along the shore were now resorting to burning the bodies in large piles.

When he arrived at the infirmary, a few of the Sisters greeted him and asked him for news. He walked right past them and into the main building. A few of the Sisters followed him in.

"Zachary, oh good heavens, we've been on pins and needles!" Mother Mechtilde exclaimed as he entered. "How are the orphans? The Sisters? Were you able to meet with Mother Camillus?"

Zachary looked at Mother Mechtilde with tears in his eyes as he struggled to form his words.

"Mother Mechtilde," he said, and the tears spilled down his face. "It's gone. There's nothing left at all!"

Mother Mechtilde's mouth opened in shock.

"The children . . . the Sisters . . . they're nowhere to be found! All gone! It's as though a broom has swept the land clean! Like it never existed!"

Mother Mechtilde slowly brought up her hands and placed them on Zachary's shoulders, pulling him into an embrace.

"My poor orphans! My poor Sisters are lost!"

Fort Crockett, which overlooked the Gulf at Forty-Fifth Street, was hit hard by the storm. Twenty-nine of its 129 soldiers were lost, and nearly all its tents were washed away. In one of the barracks left standing, Frank sat wrapped in a bedsheet on the side of a bunk bed. He looked over at William and Albert, who were clad in army uniforms, as they lay asleep in nearby beds.

A young army private entered the barracks carrying another uniform. The private had cut down uniforms for William and Albert, and now Frank's was ready. The private, himself looking like he could use some rest, sat down next to Frank on the bed.

"Try this out, buddy," he said.

Frank tossed off the bedsheet and took the uniform from the private. His body was covered with cuts and bruises and had been burned by the sun.

"It won't fit perfect," the private said as the boy dressed himself. "But I reckon it'll fit you good enough."

Frank dressed quickly and looked at the private for his approval. Even with the cutting down, Frank's arms were swallowed up by the sleeves.

The private chuckled.

"Well, maybe a little less than great, but better than no good, huh?"

Frank nodded and sat back down.

The private stood up to leave. "We're gonna get you boys to the hospital as soon as we can. We've got some men out looking for a wagon right now. You get some rest, OK?"

Frank nodded again. Then he reclined back on the bed. The uniform was way too big for him, and he had to hold on to it as he moved on the bed so that the shirt didn't slip off his shoulders. But even though the dry cloth felt like sandpaper against his skin, after so many long hours in the water, he was just thankful to be dry. Frank pressed the wounds on his head again and flinched.

Suddenly Albert sat up in his bed, his eyes still closed, and screamed Maggie's name. Frank shook, and William opened his eyes, which were red from multiple popped blood vessels.

William didn't have the strength to sit up and just lay there with his eyes open, staring at the ceiling.

Albert sat up for a few moments, his eyes still closed, and breathed heavily. His face was red from the sun and covered in cuts. Soon he fell back to sleep, still sitting up. Frank rolled off of his bed and over to Albert, gently laid his hands on Albert's shoulders, and guided him back down to his pillow. Albert then sank into a deep sleep.

Frank went back to his bed and climbed in. His head ached. And the quiet in the barracks was hard to get used to.

Even worse, he couldn't close his eyes. When he did, all he could hear was one terrible, solid scream of a hundred children.

EPILOGUE

The city of Galveston is wrapped in sackcloth
and ashes. She sits beside her unnumbered dead and refuses
to be comforted. Her sorrow and suffering are beyond
description. Her grief is unspeakable.

—Associated Press dispatch, September 10

THE WEEK AFTER THE STORM, on September 13, Daisy Thorne married Dr. Joe Gilbert in Galveston's Grace Episcopal Church, which was still caked with mud. They settled in Austin, Texas, where Dr. Gilbert continued to practice medicine. Daisy often accompanied Dr. Gilbert on his evening rounds, a practice she would continue for nearly half a century. They had one son and two daughters.

Samuel Young's wife and children received the telegram he had sent on Saturday morning, and they remained in San Antonio until the storm was over. The Youngs lived in Galveston until around 1910. After that point their name no longer appeared in the Galveston city directory. Nothing is known about Sam and his family after their departure from Galveston.

After the storm Frank Madera, Albert Campbell, and William Murney went their separate ways and lost touch. Albert moved to Topeka, Kansas, to live with his sister and her husband. He eventually ended up in California, where he became a jack of all trades, working as a pipe fitter for the Rock Island and Santa Fe Railroads and serving as a building engineer in Los Angeles. He died in 1955.

William obtained a position as an apprentice machinist for the railroad at age sixteen. He later moved to Springfield, Missouri, and worked for the Missouri Pacific Railroad. He died in 1971. Frank moved from family to family in the Houston area, served in World War I, and eventually settled in Sims Bayou, just outside the Houston city limits.

Frank reconnected with William in 1913, and they would occasionally write to each other. Neither one was able to locate Albert until a 1937 article in the *Houston Post* about their survival story, in which Frank was interviewed. A friend of Albert's saw the article, and Frank and Albert were able to meet again in Los Angeles shortly afterward. Frank died in 1953, and the three survivors were never able to have the reunion they had longed for.

———•◦•———

Even to this day the Galveston hurricane of September 8, 1900, remains the deadliest natural disaster in the history of the United States. Approximately eight thousand men, women, and children lost their lives—in other words, about one in six Galvestonians are believed to have died, either in the hurricane or in the flood that followed.

In the days after the storm, Galvestonians loaded bodies onto wagons and then piled them onto steamers to be buried at sea, but to their horror, the corpses began to wash ashore. As a result the city had to resort to burning all bodies for fear of pestilence.

The storm also decimated more than twenty-six hundred

Memorial to the hurricane victims at the Galveston Island Seawall

houses and caused more than twenty million dollars in damage (in 1900 dollars), making it second only to Hurricane Katrina in 2005 as the costliest hurricane in American history.

Before the hurricane Galveston was a boomtown. The largest city in the state of Texas at that time, Galveston was a center of trade and known nationwide as "the Wall Street of the southwest." The hurricane was a devastating blow, not only to the people of Galveston but to the city's economy, as well. A few months after the storm, oil was discovered in Beaumont, Texas. The main beneficiary of the resulting wealth was Houston, Galveston's main rival for national and international port traffic. As Galveston was still picking up the pieces after the disaster, Houston emerged as the go-to destination for ships docking in the southwest.

Nevertheless, Galveston reemerged in the twentieth century as a popular coastal city for tourists. Every February, for example, more than two hundred fifty thousand people visit Galveston to celebrate the city's Mardi Gras festival. To guard against another catastrophe, construction on a seawall began in September 1902, and the first segment, which stretched 3.3 miles, was completed in 1904. By 1963, the seawall stretched more than ten miles along the shore.

The Sisters of Charity of the Incarnate Word continues as a multicultural international ministry, now based in Houston. On September 8, wherever they are in the world—whether it is in their ministries in El Salvador, Guatemala, Ireland, Kenya, or the United States—the Sisters of Charity sing "Queen of the Waves," a hymn that has been sung on that date every year to commemorate the lives lost at the orphanage in 1900.

Author's Note

Like most authors of historical fiction, I faced many challenges in creating this novel. History, after all, is sprawling and untidy and, very often, incomplete. There are many accounts of the Galveston hurricane—in the form of memoirs, interviews, letters, and so on. But details are often hard to come by and must be filled in, especially those involving people who didn't survive.

The true account of St. Mary's Orphanage, for example, can only be told by the three young survivors—William, Albert, and Frank—and these three men, unfortunately, left only a basic record of their remembrances of that night. Provided with the brief accounts given by the three boys to news media, I had to rely heavily upon the records of the Congregation of the Sisters of Charity of the Incarnate Word, the details of contemporary accounts, and, ultimately, my own imagination. I also had to fill in portions of the Lucas Terrace and Samuel Young story lines, based on the limited information available. Additionally, it is impossible to know all the conversations that took place amongst the characters, so a certain amount of imagined dialogue was necessary in order to bring the narrative alive.

It's an unfortunate fact that there are no firsthand accounts of the Galveston disaster by African Americans. In a social sense, Galveston was quite racially integrated for its time, but it was still, like much of the United States, geographically segregated. African Americans, therefore, died in tragically disproportionate numbers in Galveston, because they generally resided in the zone of total destruction, south of Broadway, towards the beach. I felt strongly that my story of the Galveston hurricane could not be told without any African American voices. I wanted to provide as realistic a glimpse as possible into the lives of Galvestonians of the time and what they went through on that tragic night. This is why I included the characters of Charlie, who worked for Sam Young, and Leonard and Jerome, who brought Young out of the storm. Dr. Young's own account of the hurricane mentions a black man who worked for him and whom he sent home on Saturday morning when the weather started looking grim. The man remains nameless in Dr. Young's account and is not remarked upon further. Because there was very little to go on beyond this fleeting mention, the character of Charlie is largely an invention on my part—one I felt necessary to include. Also nameless in Dr. Young's account are those African Americans who helped him into the house where they were taking shelter. I decided to highlight two of them in order to depict those scenes realistically, so I created the characters of Leonard and Jerome.

Photo Credits

Cover and Chapter Opener
Courtesy of Library of Congress

Chapter 1
Page 7: Courtesy of Archives of the Congregation of the Sisters of Charity of the Incarnate Word, Houston, Texas
Page 12: Courtesy of Archives of the Congregation of the Sisters of Charity of the Incarnate Word, Houston, Texas

Chapter 2
Page 17: Courtesy of Archives of the Congregation of the Sisters of Charity of the Incarnate Word, Houston, Texas
Page 23: Courtesy of Archives of the Congregation of the Sisters of Charity of the Incarnate Word, Houston, Texas

Chapter 3
Page 31: Courtesy of the Rosenberg Library, Galveston, Texas

Chapter 4
Page 46: Courtesy of Archives of the Congregation of the Sisters of Charity of the Incarnate Word, Houston, Texas

Chapter 6
Page 68: Courtesy of Library of Congress

Chapter 7
Page 79: Courtesy of Library of Congress

Chapter 8
Page 97: Courtesy of Library of Congress

Chapter 9
Page 105: Courtesy of Library of Congress
Page 108: Courtesy of Library of Congress

Chapter 10
Page 113: Courtesy of Library of Congress
Page 118: Courtesy of Library of Congress
Page 121: Courtesy of Library of Congress

Epilogue
Page 127: Courtesy of Galveston Tourism Board